THE
AGE OF THE IMPERIAL GUPTAS

The Manindra Chandra Nandy Lectures, 1924
(Revised by the author in 1929—30)

THE
AGE OF THE IMPERIAL GUPTAS

The Late Prof. R. D. Banerji, M.A.

Manindra Chandra Nandy, Professor of Ancient Indian History and Culture, Benares Hindu University.
Formerly, Archaeological Superintendent.
Eastern Circle, Calcutta

GYAN

Published by

Gyan Publishing House
5, Ansari Road
Daryaganj, New Delhi-110002
Phone: 011-47034999, 9811692060
E-mail: books@gyanbooks.com

Distribution Network
gyanbooks.com
India, USA, Canada, UK, Australia, France

ISBN : 978-81-212-2608-0 (HB)
First Published, 1933

2nd Impression 2021

Printed at: Gyan Press, Delhi.

The
Age of the Imperial Guptas
Author: R. D. Banerji

The Manindra Chandra Nandy Lectures, 1924.

(Revised by the author in 1929—30)

THE AGE OF THE IMPERIAL GUPTAS.

BY

THE LATE PROF. R. D. BANERJI, M. A.,

Manindra Chandra Nandy Professor of Ancient Indian History and Culture, Benares Hindu University.

Formerly, Archæological Superintendent, Eastern Circle, Calcutta.

PUBLISHED BY THE BENARES HINDU UNIVERSITY.

1933.

PREFACE.

The following six lectures on the "Age of the Imperial Guptas" were delivered at the Hindu University by the late Prof. R. D. Banerji in November, 1924. Owing to his other preoccupations, Mr. Banerji was unable to take up the work of publishing his lectures till he eventually joined the Benares Hindu University as Manindra Chandra Nandy Professor of Ancient Indian History and Culture in 1928. The author revised the manuscript in 1929 and brought the work up-to-date. Five chapters of the book were also printed off when Mr. Banerji suddenly died in May, 1930, to the great regret of the learned world. Two proofs of the last chapter were seen by the author, but he did not live to give the print order.

The sudden death of Prof. Banerji naturally created further difficulties in expediting the publication of the work. A good deal of time was required to prepare the necessary blocks, the idea of incorporating them having obviously occured to the author at a late stage of printing. Permission had also to be obtained of the Archæological authorities for the utilisation of some of the photographs.

The Age of the Imperial Guptas is a very important epoch in Ancient Indian History and the need of a handy volume dealing with the history and many-sided aetivities of the age was long felt. Some writers have dealt with the political history of the period. Others have contributed a few notes discussing some of the problems of the Gupta Administration. But no book has been so far published which delineates with a masterly hand the multifarious manifestations of the spirit of the age. The late professor Banerji has attempted this task in these lectures, and the reader will find in the following pages an account not only of the Gupta chronology and administration but also of the literary and religious revival, and of the architectural, sculptural and numismatic achievements of the age. The book is far from being a mere compilation ; the author has suggested a number of new and interesting solutions of several controversial problems in the political and administrative history of the period, and his treatment of the architecture and plastic arts of the age, coming as it does from the masterly pen of the mature archæologist, will be found to be particularly fresh and illuminating. This was the last book to be finished by the late Prof. Banerji and it will be found to be doing ample justice to his mature and brilliant talents. It is a great pity that Prof. Banerji should not have been spared to see the publication of his lectures.

The Benares Hindu University is very much indebted to the Government of India and to the Director General of Archæology in India for giving permission to reproduce the pictures from which plates Nos. 2, 4 and 20 have been prepared, and to utilise a few other photographs which the late Prof. Banerji had obtained from Archæological Survey offices.

Benares Hindu University.
31-3-1933.

A. S. ALTEKAR,
Manindra Chandra Nandy Professor of Ancient Indian History and Culture

CONTENTS.

LIST OF ILLUSTRATIONS.

CHAPTER I.

The Chronology.

The century which preceded the final rise of Magadha as the leader of the nations of Northern India is yet one of the darkest periods of Indian History. The series of epigraphs which illustrate the history of the Imperial Great Kuṣāṇas at Mathuāa end abruptly towards the close of the second century A.D. For Western India we possess an almost complete series of dated coins of the later Western Kṣatrapas, for the Panjab we have the coins of the Later Great Kuṣāṇas and the Kidāras, but for Eastern India we possess nothing. In the beginning of the fourth century A.D., a strong flood of light is suddenly thrown on the history of North Eastern India with the rise of the Gupta dynasty. Nothing is known about the antecedents of Candragupta I except that his ancestors were petty landholders with the rank of *Mahārāja*. In the fourth century A.D., this title had ceased to denote the Imperial rank or even that of an independent prince and had been bestowed on provincial governors by the later emperors of the Gupta dynasty. Some writers even suppose that the ancestors of Candragupta I were people of humble origin and even the humble title of *Mahārāja* had been bestowed upon them as an act of courtesy by the subordinates and officials of Candragupta's son Samudragupta.

What was the condition of Magadha when under the leadership of Candragupta I the people of that country attained independence and later on suzerainty? Magadha had been annexed to the Kuṣāṇa empire in the first century A.D., by the generals of Kāṇiṣka I and the venerated alms-bowl of the Buddha taken away from Vaiśālī to Puruṣapura or Peshawar. In the year 3 of the era of Kāṇiṣka, *i.e.*, in 81 A.D., a Kuṣāṇa Great-Satrap (*Mahākṣatrapa*) named Kharapāllaṇa was ruling over North Eastern India and under him there was a governor or Satrap (*Kṣatrapa*) named Vanaspara,[1] probably in charge of the provinces of the extreme North East, extending from Benares to Eastern Bengal. It is, therefore, quite probable that even in the opening decades of the fourth century A.D., North Eastern India was being ruled by a Scythian Great Satrap and Magadha by a Satrap. The coinage, both gold and copper, of the Later Great Kushans is still extremely abundant in the markets of Patna, Gaya and Benares and on this evidence alone, in the absence of others, it would be pertinent to assume that the Later Great Kushans continued to rule over North Eastern India. The foundation of an independent kingdom in Magadha by Candragupta I, therefore, amounted to the

[1] *Epigraphia Indica, Vol. VIII, pp. 176, 179.*

liberation of the people of Magadha from the thraldom of the hated Scythian foreigner.

We can assume that Candragupta, the son of Ghaṭotkacagupta, and the grandson of Śrīgupta, assumed the leadership of the citizens of Pāṭaliputra and the people of Magadha in this war of independence. The different steps are not known to us but some of them may be guessed with a certain amount of accuracy. It is certain that neither Śrīgupta nor his son Ghaṭotkacagupta were people of much importance in the country. Hariṣeṇa, one of the ministers of Samudragupta, calls them Mahārājas but the title had declined very much in importance. It had ceased to be an Imperial title. The Great Aśoka was content with the title of *Rājan*. The Greeks introduced the first change when they translated the title "*Basileus Basileuon*" and the Persian "*Shāhanshāh*" into *Mahārāja-Rājātirāja*. Under the Imperial Great Kushans several additions were made to the Imperial title such as *Devaputra* in imitation of the title "Son of Heaven" of the Emperors of China. Early in the fourth century the Imperial title expanded into *Parameśvara-Paramabhaṭṭāraka-Mahārājādhirāja*. In the reign of Kumāragupta I we find that the governors of Northern Bengal, though not of royal descent and holding the rank of *Uparika*, are styled *Mahārājas*.[1] Therefore we may

[1] *Epigraphia Indica, Vol. XV, pp 138.*

assume that the ancestors of Candragupta I were people of no very great importance in Magadha. Whether they were subordinate chiefs with the title of *Mahārājas* or mere nonentities to whom Hariṣeṇa gave the rank of *Mahārājas* out of courtsey, need not trouble us. We learn from the coins of Candragupta I or those ascribed to him, but really issued by his son and successor Samudragupta, that Candragupta acquired importance by his marriage with the Licchavi princess Kumāradevī. So much emphasis is given to the Lichchhavī connection by Samudragupta that there cannot be any doubt about its importance. On the coins of Candragupta I, which Allan takes to be memorial medals struck by Samudragupta in honour of his parents, we see Candragupta I and Kumāradevī standing side by side with their names struck separately. On the reverse we find the word "*Licchavayaḥ*," in the plural number, which cannot be explained unless the Guptas are also taken to be descended from Licchavī oligarchs. The Licchavīs were, originally, inhabitants of Northern Bihar or Tīrabhukti, with their capital at Vaiśālī. They were ruled by a number of oligarchs selected from certain families only. They were a powerful nation whose depredations in the country to the south of the Ganges compelled the kings of Magadha to build a strong fort at the confluence of that river with the Son, which became the nucleus of the great city of Pāṭaliputra. The independence of the Licchavī oligarchy was subsequently destroyed by Ajātaśatru, king of Magadha. Subsequently the Licchavīs migrated to or conquered Nepal in the early mediæval period.

Strengthened by the Licchavī alliance Candragupta I was able either to drive out the Scythian Satrap of Magadha or to throw off the loose allegiance of the chiefs of Magadha to the Later Great Kuṣāṇas of Mathurā or the Panjab. Candragupta I was most probably advanced in years at the time of the revolution or the war of independence in Magadha and we have positive proof of his short rule in the date of the Gaya copper plate inscription of his son, Samudragupta. He simply drove out the Scythians and gave independence to the province of Magadha after three centuries of subjection and foreign oppression.

The restoration of independence to Magadha was no doubt due to a revival of national spirit in that province and Candragupta I was merely the leader of the band of heroes who accomplished the feat. Prior to the Sātavāhana conquest of Magadha in the first century B.C., that country was the predominant power in India. From the time of the kings of Nanda dynasty the lead of Magadha had been unquestionably recognised by all nations of Northern India and its capital, Pāṭaliputra had become the metropolis of India. The power of its kings had struck terror into the hearts of the victorious legionaries of Alexander the Great and the

Greek phalanxes with their myriads of auxilliaries had retired from the western frontier of the empire of Magadha before risking an engagement. Another Magadhan Emperor had caused Seleukos Nikator to retire with humbled pride after ceding the fairest Asiatic provinces of Alexander's Empire. A third emperor, the successful Brāhmaṇa general, Pushyamitra had tried in vain to stem the tide of repeated Greek invasions from Bactria and Afghanistan. The repeated treachery of the Brāhmaṇa ministers of Magadha at last laid the people of Magadha prostrate at the feet of Dravidian conqueror and after the Sātavāhana conquest Magadha ceased to be the leader of Indian nations and Pāṭaliputra, the metropolis of India.

Magadha rose after four centuries of slumber, once more to take its place in the vanguard of national armies and its rise again brought independence, self-realization and glory to the people of Northern India. Once again Magadha became the mistress of an empire which extended from the Western to the Eastern sea and from the foot of Himalayas to the banks of Narmadā.

Even after a century of discussion scholars are not yet agreed about the correct date of the war of independence in Magadha. The late Dr. J. F. Fleet came to the conclusion that Magadha became independent in 319-20 A.D., and the era, which is now known to us as the Gupta or the Gupta-Valabhī era was founded by the Licchavis of

Nepal,[1] Candragupta I. Subsequently the late Dr. Bühler proved that the era which became subsequently known as the Gupta era was really founded from the date of the coronation of Candragupta I.[2] There cannot be any doubt about the fact that the initial year of the Gupta era corresponds to 319-20 A.D. In the absence of fresh data it is impossible to decide finally what was the real cause of the foundation of this era. It is quite possible that the Licchavīs who were close relations of the Guptas, used the era counted from the liberation of the people of Magadha.

One important factor was lost sight of at the time of the decision of the point. The Gaya copper plate of Samudragupta, issued in the 9th year of his reign was regarded as spurious by the late Dr. J. F. Fleet. When his work was published our knowledge of Indian Epigraphy was not so extensive as it is now. Our knowledge of the form of Imperial Gupta land-grants was limited to the Indor-khera inscribed copper plate of the time of the emperor Skandagupta in 1883. The Natore or Dhanaidaha plate of Kumāragupta I, the six Damodarpur plates of the emperors Kumāragupta I, Budhagupta and Bhānugupta and finally the three Faridpur plates of the kings Dharmāditya and Gopachandra have thrown a flood of light on the procedure of issuing grants of land or deeds recording transfers of the same. In the

[1] *Gupta Inscriptions, Introduction, p. 22.*

[2] *Vienna Oriental Journal, Vol. V, 1891, pp. 217-29.*

face of this mass of new evidence it is impossible to believe at the present day that the Gaya copper plate grant of the 9th year of Samudragupta is forged. It cannot be regarded as spurious in the same light as the Sudi plates and in the writer's opinion it is genuine. According to the established custom to be found in Gupta inscriptions, we should regard the date of this inscription as one expressed in the Gupta era; *i.e.*, it was issued in 328-29 A.D. If Samudragupta was reigning in the 9th year of this era then it would be more natural to suppose that this era was counted from the date of the accession of Samudragupta's father, Candragupta I, the liberator of the people of Magadha, who, according to a consensus of opinion amongst scholars, died after a very short reign.

According to the latest interpretation of the numismatic evidence Samudragupta struck a number of commemorative medals during his reign and the coins which were hitherto regarded as the regular issues of Candragupta I are now regarded as medals struck in memory of his parents by Samudragupta. Numismatists have not been able to account for gold coins issued by a king or prince named Kāca. In execution these coins are allied to the group of memorial medals issued by Samudragupta and therefore Mr. J. Allan of the British Museum is inclined to regard them as issues of Samudragupta. But up to this time coins of the same Gupta king bearing two different names in addition to the *birudas* or the *Āditya*-name have not been discovered. The established practice of Gupta coins is to put the real name of the king on the margin of the obverse or at the foot of the royal figure in a vertical line and his *birudas* on the reverse or elsewhere. All different types of the coins of Samudragupta, Candragupta II, Kumāragupta I and Skandagupta show the actual name of the king on the obverse either in the margin or at the foot of the royal figure on gold coins. Regarded in this light the group of extremely rare gold coins bearing the name Kāca are either issues of some other prince of that name or memorial medals struck by Samudragupta for a relative of that name. Who this prince was we do not know. Was he another son of Candragupta I whose reign had intervened between those of Candragupta I and Samudragupta? If the coins bearing the name of Kāca are real coins and not medals then Kāca was most probably the elder brother of Samudragupta whose rule was very short. But if they are medals struck in the memory of a relative by Samudragupta then Kāca was most probably another son of Candragupta I, who had lost his life in the war of independence. Gupta inscriptions generally omit the name of a prince who is not in the direct line of succession. The Bhitari seal of Kumāragupta II omits the name of the emperor Skandagupta, the elder brother of Puragupta. For this reason it is easier to account for the omission of the name of Kāca in the genealogical tables of Gupta inscriptions. It is more probable that coins bearing the name of Kāca are memorial medals because Hariṣeṇa, the official historiographer of the reign of Samudragupta, states in the Allahabad pillar inscription that he (Samudragupta) was elected the heir-apparent (*yuvarāja*) during the life time of his father. Kāca, therefore, appears to be a son of Candragupta I who had lost his life during the life time of his father very probably in the war of independence.

Candragupta I left Magadha independent but a minor power in the political arena of Northern India in the 4th century A.D. Either in his lifetime or shortly afterwards a king of the Indian Desert, Candravarman of Puṣkaraṇā, overran the whole of Northern India from Eastern Bengal to the seven mouths of Indus. The statements of the inscription on the iron pillar now standing in the Masjid Qūwwat-ul-Islām at Meherauli[1] have been partly corroborated by the discovery of another inscription on the Susunia rock in the western part of the Bankura district.[2] In this inscription Candravarman calls himself a king of Puṣkaraṇā, and informs us that his father's name was Mahārāja Siṁhavarman. Hariṣeṇa in his Allahabad pillar inscription tells us that Candravarman was one of the kings of Northern India

---

1 Fleet—*Gupta inscriptions ; Corpus Inscriptionum Indicarum, Vol. III, p. 141.*

2 *Epi. Ind. Vol. XIII, p. 133 ; Vol. XIV, pp. 367–71.*

vanquished by Samudragupta. Candravarman's younger brother Naravarman was ruling over Mandasor, the ancient Daśapura, as an independent ruler in V.S. 461=404 A.D.,[1] i.e., even after the conquest of Mālava by Candragupta II. Naravarman's son and successor Viśvavarman did not acknowledge the suzerainty of the emperor Kumāragupta in V.S. 480=424 A.D.,[2] but Naravarman's grandson Bandhuvarman openly acknowledged the suzerainty of Kumāragupta I in his Mandasor inscription of V.S. 493=436-37 A.D.[3] The campaign of Candravarman in Northern India appears to have taken place before Samudragupta's conquest of the same region. We do not know what happened in the newly founded kingdom of Magadha during this campaign. It is also possible that Candravarman's campaign took place before the accession of Candragupta I and at the same time it is quite probable that Candragupta I was defeated by Candravarman because in order to reach Susunia in Western Bengal the latter must have passed through Magadha.

Samudragupta, one of the younger sons of Candragupta I was marked out for his abilities and selected as the heir-apparent by his father. Soon after the death of Candragupta I, Samudragupta started to consolidate his power by conquering the small principalities into which Northern India had become divided at that time. The

1 *Ibid. Vol. XII, pp. 315-21.*

2 *Gupta Inscriptions pp. 72-78.*

3 *Ibid. pp. 79-88.*

Allahabad pillar inscription of Hariṣeṇa mentions two kings named Acyuta and Nāgasena, at first along with a chief of the Kota tribe, whose name has been lost. We do not know who Nāgasena was but Acyuta[1] and the Kota[2] tribe are both known from small copper coins issued by them. Nāgasena and Acyuta are mentioned once more among a number of kings of *Āryāvarta* or Northern India, who were totally destroyed by Samudragupta; proving thereby that both Acyuta and the Kota tribe belonged to Northern India. The coins of Acyuta are to be found only at Ramnagar near Aonla in the Bareilly district, the site of the ancient Ahicchatra, the ancient capital of Northern Pañcāla. Therefore Acyuta may be taken to be a king of the Pañcala country. The little known coins of the Kota tribe are said to be very common in Delhi and the Eastern Panjab and the Kotas therefore may be taken to be a tribe of North Eastern Rajputana. Hariṣeṇa in his Allahabad pillar inscription introduces the kings of Southern India defeated by Samudragupta after mentioning Nāgasena, Acyuta and the Kota tribe but before bringing in the kings of Northern India uprooted by that monarch. The kings of Āryāvarta mentioned in l.21 of Allahabad pillar inscription are:—1. Rudradeva, 2. Matila, 3. Nāgadatta, 4. Candravarman,

---

[1] *J.R.A.S. 1897, pp. 420, 862; Indian Museum Catalogue Vol. I. pp. 185, 188-89.*

[2] *Ibid. pp. 258, 264.*

5. Gaṇapatināga, 6. Nāgasena, 7. Acyuta, 8. Nandin, and 9. Balavarman. Out of these nine chiefs Rudradeva, Nāgadatta, Nāgasena, Nandin and Balavarman are not known to us from any other source. Matila is known from a clay seal discovered in Bulandshahr.[1] Candravarman is known to us from the Meherauli iron pillar inscription and the Susunia rock inscription. Gaṇapatināga is known from his coins[2] and appears to have been a king of the Nāga tribe of Nalapura, modern Narwar in Gwalior State. Rapson has proposed to identify Nāgasena with a prince of the same name mentioned in the Harṣacarita of Bāṇa.[3] The identification of Rudradeva, Nāgadatta and Nandin is not possible without fresh materials. Balavarman may be the king of Assam of that name who was ninth in ascent from Bhāskaravarman, the contemporary of Harṣavardhana and Yuan Chwang, and the grandson of Puṣyavarman, the founder of the dynasty.[4] If we except Balavarman and the unidentified princes then we find that the kings of Āryāvarta defeated by Samudragupta were mostly rulers of North Western and Central India. Acyuta belonged to the Bareilly district, Matila to the Bulandshahr district, Gaṇapatināga to Narwar or Pawāyā or Padmāvatī in the Gwalior State, the Kotas to North Eastern Rajputana and Candra-

[1] *Ind. Ant. Vol. XVIII, 1889, p. 289.*

[2] *Indian Museum Catalogue Vol. I. pp. 164, 178–79.*

[3] *J.R.A.S. 1898, p. 449.*

[4] *Epi. Ind. Vol. XII. p. 69.*

varman to Pokharan in Southern Rajputana. Only the district around Agra and Delhi and Panjab are not mentioned. So also are omitted the kings of the different parts of Bengal, if there were any left after the foundation of the Gupta kingdom by Candragupta I.

The mention of the kings defeated by Samudragupta in his southern campaign before those of Āryāvarta or Northern India may indicate that the Southern campaign was undertaken immediately after the defeat of Nāgasena, Acyuta and the Kotas; but it would perhaps be difficult to believe that a great general like Samudragupta departed for Southern India leaving so many powerful enemies in his rear. The kings defeated by him in his southern campaign are :—

1. Mahendra of Kośala or the Bilaspur and Raipur districts of the Central Provinces.
2. Vyāghrarāja of Mahākāntāra or the great forest (Eastern Gondwana).
3. Maṇṭarāja of Koraḷa.
4. Mahendra of Piṣṭapura or modern Pittapuram in the Godavarī district of the Madras Presidency.
5. Svāmidatta of Giri-Koṭṭura.
6. Damana of Eraṇḍapalla.
7. Viṣṇugopa of Kāñcī or Conjeeveram in the Chingleput district.
8. Nīlarāja of Avamukta.
9. Hastivarman of Veṅgī.
10. Ugrasena of Pālakka.

11. Kubera of Devarāṣṭra.
12. Dhanañjaya of Kusthalapura.

Even in 1883 there could not be any doubt about the identification of Kośala, Piṣṭapura, Kāñcī, and Veṅgī. The late Drs. Fleet and V. A. Smith proposed to identify Pālakka with Palghat on the Malabar coast. Smith subsequently found out that Pālakka was the name of a place in the Nellore district.[1] Devarāṣṭra and Eraṇḍapalla have all along been identified by both of these scholars with Mahārāṣṭra and Erandol in the East Khandesh district of the Bombay Presidency. The earlier theory that Pālakka was Pālghat was feasible at that time, but with the discovery of Pālakka in the Nellore district it became difficult to understand how Samudragupta could conquer Mahārāṣṭra and Khandesh without passing through and conquering the intervening Kanarese districts. It remained for a French scholar to clear up the mystery about the places and kings of Southern India mentioned in the Allahabad Pillar inscription. M. Jouveau-Dubreuil of the Colonial College, Pondicherry[2] identified these places correctly. He has proved that Eraṇḍapallī is the name of a place mentioned in the Siddhantam plates of Devendravarman of Kaliṅga.[3] Devarāṣṭra is mentioned as the name of a district or province in Kaliṅga in a

[1] *Early History of India. 4th Edition p. 301.*

[2] *Ancient History of the Deccan, Eng. Trans. Pondicherry 1920, pp. 58–61.*

[3] *Epi. Ind. Vol. XII pp. 212.*

set of copper plates discovered in Kasimkota in the Vizagapatam district. With Pālakka in the Nellore district and Eraṇḍapallī and Devarāṣṭra on the Eastern Coast, the probability of a wide southern conquest by Samudragupta became almost impossible. But though Pālakka is acknowledged to be in the Nellore district writers on Ancient Indian History have not yet given up their original ideas.[1]

Among the twelve places mentioned in the Allahabad pillar inscription, the princes of which were vanquished by Samudragupta, Koraḷa, Avamukta and Kusthalapura cannot be identified even now. But the position of the remaining nine clearly indicates the route of Samudragupta's march. He passed through the Rewah State and the Jubbulpur district, defeated Mahendra of Mahakośala, entered the Eastern Gondwana forest, where he defeated a chief named Vyāghrarāja and emerged on the eastern coast in the Vizagapatam district. The Vyāghrarāja mentioned in the Allahabad pillar inscription appears to be the same as that mentioned in the Nachne-ki-talai[2] and Ganj[3] inscriptions of the Vākāṭaka Mahārāja Pṛthivīsena I. Mr. K. N. Dikshit, Superintendent of the Archæological Survey of India, Eastern Circle is certainly wrong in ascribing these two inscriptions to Pṛthivīsena II.[4] The Poona plates

---

1 V. A. Smith's *Early History of India, 4th Edition p. 301.*

2 *Gupta Inscriptions, p. 234.*

3 *Epi. Ind. Vol. XVII. p. 13.* 4 *Ibid. p. 362.*

of the 13th year of the queen Prabhāvatīguptā are written in a different script altogether, which does not show the use of the box-headed type of the *seriff.*[1] This particular variety of the 5th century alphabet appears to be the South-Western variety. The Ganj and Nachne-ki-talai inscriptions and the Chammak[2] and Siwani[3] plates belong to the North-Eastern variety of the Central Indian alphabet of the same century. The Ganj inscription shows well-marked box-heads on the top of letters but the Nachne-ki-talai record shows an incipient stage in the formation of the boxes. In the Balaghat plates of Pṛthivīṣeṇa III[4] we find completely developed boxes. For these reasons it is not possible to agree with M. Jouveau-Dubreuil.[5]

After emerging from the forest Samudragupta defeated Maṇṭarāja of Koraḷa and another Mahendra of Piṣṭapura; then he proceeded south and defeated Svāmidatta of Koṭṭura hill, modern Kothoor in the Ganjam district. Ugrasena of Pālakka in the Nellore district, Hastivarman of Veṅgī and Viṣṇugopa of Kāñcī were still far away, but Damana of Eraṇḍapali and Kuvera of Devarāṣṭra in the Vizagapatam district were close neighbours of Svāmidatta of Kothoor and Mahendra of Pittapuram. It appears that

---

1 *Ibid. Vol. XV. pp. 41-42.*

2 *Gupta Inscriptions, pp. 236-40.*

3 *Ibid., pp. 245-47;* see also *Ind. Ant. Vol. LV, 1926, pp. 103, 323-27.*

4 *Epi. Ind. Vol. IX, pp. 270-71.*

5 *Ancient History of the Deccan, pp. 72-73.*

Samudragupta was opposed by a confederacy of Pallava kings headed by Viṣṇugopa of Kāñcī, and Hastivarman of Veṅgī. M. Jouveau-Dubreuil is of opinion that "Samudragupta first subjugated some kings, but that very soon he encountered superior forces and was therefore obliged to relinquish his conquests and return rapidly to his own state."[1] It is not possible to corroborate this statement. Samudragupta's southern campaign was of the nature of a *Dig-vijaya* and therefore the question of the capitulation of conquered territories does not arise. On the other hand it is quite probable that Samudragupta advanced as far as Veṅgī and Kāñcī and defeated Hastivarman and Viṣṇugopa. M. Jouveau-Dubreuil has succeeded in proving that Samudragupta never went beyond Kāñcī and his supposed conquest of the Coimbator and Malabar districts of the Madras Presidency and the Mahārāṣṭra and Khandesh are myths. The Allahabad pillar inscription does not supply us with any other materials except the names of Samudragupta's neighbours and some traits of his personal character. This inscription does not mention one important event of the king's reign. After his conquests the great king performed the Aśvamedha ceremony: but we know of this event from his coins and one inscription of one of his successors. Special coins or medals were struck by Samudragupta, more

---

[1] *Ibid, p. 60.*

probably for distributions among the Brāhmaṇas attending or taking part in that ceremony. On these coins the king styles himself *Aśvamedha-parākramaḥ*,[1] "Powerful enough to have performed the ceremony of the sacrifice of the horse."

We can deduce the limits of Samudragupta's kingdom from the Allahabad pillar and other inscriptions. No part of Southern or Western India was included in his dominions. The discovery of the Poona plates of Prabhāvatīguptā has established the fact that the Ganj and Nachna inscriptions cannot be assigned to the 7th century A.D. The mention of Vyāghra proves that Pṛthivīṣeṇa I, the grandfather of Pravarasena II, was the contemporary of Samudragupta. Nachna and Ganj are both situated in the heart of ancient Ḍābhāla or Ḍāhala and therefore it seems certain that the country to the south of the Jumna was not included in the dominions of Samudragupta. The districts lying to the south Vindhyas were included in the Vākāṭaka kingdom. There is one exception to this. The Eran inscription of Samudragupta proves that the north-eastern corner of Malwa, at least, was in his occupation. According to this inscription Samudragupta established some monuments at this place, then known as Airakiṇa, now a village in the Sagar district of the Central Provinces.[2] We have no proof of the extension of Samudragupta's kingdom into

[1] *British Museum Catalogue of Indian Coins : Gupta dynasties*, p. 21.
[2] *Gupta Inscriptions*, pp. 18-20.

the heart of Mālava. The countries and tribes mentioned in the Allahabad pillar inscription of Samudragupta indicate the limits of the zone of Samudragupta's influence pretty accurately. Kings of Samataṭa, Ḍavāka, Kāmarūpa, Nepāla and Kartṛpura are mentioned as princes on the frontiers (*pratyanta-nṛpati*). Of these names only Ḍavāka cannot be definitely located; Samataṭa is South-Eastern Bengal, Kāmarūpa is lower Assam, Nepāla is the valley of the same name and Kartṛpura the Kangra valley. Therefore the empire of Samudragupta was bounded on the East by the Delta of the Ganges and Assam and on the North by the valleys of Nepāl and Kangra. Ḍavāka is generally taken to be Dacca. But according to another theory it may be the ancient kingdom of Tagaung in upper Burma. Therefore the Northern part of the Ganges Delta may have been included in the empire of Samudragupta. In the same place of the Allahabad pillar inscription a number of tribes are mentioned.—1. Mālavas, 2. Arjunāyanas, 3. Yaudheyas, 4. Mādrakas, 5. Ābhīras, 6. Prārjunas, 7. Sanakānīkas, 8. Kākas and 9. Kharaparikas. Among these tribes the Mālavas and Yaudheyas can be located correctly but others cannot be properly identified or located. The Mālavas are decidedly the Malloi of Alexander's historians; they have given their name to more than one district and country in India, *e.g.*, Mālava and Malwa. To-day there is a Malwa in the South Eastern Punjab and the ancient Mughal *Ṣubah* of Mālwā is now included in the dominions of the Śindes of Gwalior and the Hoḷkars of Indore. The Mālavas are known from their copper coins to have continued to exist as a tribal republic for nearly four centuries. These copper coins are to be found over a very large area beginning from a valley of the Sutlej down to the banks of Narmadā. According to Cunningham the age of these coins range from 250 B.C., to 350 A.D. The earliest of them were issued in the name of the tribal republic of the Mālavas with the legend *Mālavānāṁ jayaḥ* [1] "Victory to the Mālavas." Some of them use the word *Gaṇa* [2] denoting that they were tribal coins of the Mālava republic. Later on they seem to have elected oligarchs or tribal kings whose names only are to be found on some of their coins. Some of these coins are assigned by Smith and Rapson to 150 B.C. Some coins bear the name of the king as well as the word Gaṇa indicating thereby that these kings were tribal kings or executive officers of the republic.[3] The Mālava tribal coinage suddenly comes to an end at the end of the 4th century.[4]

The Yaudheyas still survive in the Panjab and Sindh. They have become Musulmans and inhabit the banks of the Indus from Bahāwalpur and Multan to the Kohistān *tāluqa* of the Karachi district. Parts of the Bahāwalpur State and the

---

1 Smith—*Indian Museum Catalogue, Vol. I, pp. 170–73.*

2 *Ibid, pp. 173-74.* 3 *Ibid, p. 175. No. 72 a.* 4 *Ibid. p. 162.*

Multan district are still called Johiyāwār. Remnants of the tribe still inhabit the Kohistān *tāluqa* of the Karachi district under their own chief who is known as the *Johiyā-jo-Jām.*[1] The yaudheyas were defeated by the Mahākṣatrapa Rudrādaman I sometime before 150 A.D.[2] At one time the Yaudheyas inhabited Eastern Rajputana and one of their inscriptions of the 3rd century A.D., has been discovered at Bayana[3] in the southern part of the Bharatpur State. They are also known from their tribal coins. Some of them were issued in the name of the Yaudheya tribal republic,[4] while others bear names of kings.[5] Like the Mālava tribal coinage, the Yaudheya coinage also comes to a sudden end in the 4th century A.D.

The remaining tribes mentioned in the Allahabad pillar inscription of Samudragupta are not so well known to us. The Arjunāyanas are known from their coins only, which are exceedingly rare.[6] The joint cabinets of the Asiatic Society of Bengal and the Indian Museum contain two coins only. Their habitat is also unknown. But as their coins resemble those of the Northern Satraps and the Yaudheyas, they may tentatively be taken to be inhabitants of Northern Rajputana.[7] The Ābhīras

---

[1] An extensive cemetery of the Johiyā-jams was discovered by me at Landhi in the Karachi district. *Annual Report of the Arch. Survey of India, Western Circle for the year ending 31st March 1920*, p. 79, pl. *viii.*

[2] *Epi. Ind. Vol. VIII, p. 44.* [3] *Gupta Inscriptions p. 252.*

[4] *Indian Museum Catalogue Vol. I, pp. 182-83.*

[5] *Ibid., pp. 181-82.* [6] *Ibid., p. 166..* [7] *Ibid., p. 160.*

are known to be inhabitants of Western India and some of their kings ruled over Kathiawad.[1] Very little is known about the Madras unless they are the same as the Madras of the Vedic and Epic texts.[2] Nothing is known about the Prārjunas and the Kharaparikas. The Kharaparas are mentioned in a Damoh inscription of the 13th century.[3] The Sanakānīkas are known from an inscription of the time of Candragupta II. In the year 82 of the Gupta era a chief of this tribe caused a cave temple to be excavated in a low rock near Bhilsa in the Gwalior State.[4] The Kākas are known from tribal surnames in modern Kashmir. It appears therefore that the tribes mentioned in the Allahabad pillar inscription of Samudragupta inhabited the Southern Panjab and Northern Rajputana in the 4th century A.D.

The Allahabad pillar inscription of Samudragupta contains only one other point of interest. In line 23 it is stated that "The Daivaputras, Shāhis, Shāhānushāhis, Śakas and Muruṇḍas" as well as the people of Siṁhala submitted to Samudragupta. This particular passage cannot be properly understood as yet. We know from Kuṣāṇa inscriptions that the titles Devaputra, Ṣāhi and Ṣāhānuṣāhi were used by the Imperial Great Kuṣāṇas. In the inscription of the year 8

[1] *British Museum Catalogue of Indian Coins; Andhras. W. Kṣatrapas etc., p. cxxxiii.*

[2] *Cambridge History of India, Vol. I, pp. 121,274.*

[3] *Epi. Ind. Vol. XII, p. 46.*

[4] *Gupta Inscriptions, p. 25.*

from Mathurā Kāṇiṣka I uses the titles Mahārāja, Rājātirāja and Ṣāhi.[1] He uses the title Devaputra in a number of inscriptions.[2] This title is also used by Huviṣka.[3] While Vāsudeva I is known to have used this title at least once.[4] The title Ṣāhanuṣāhi appears to be the result of an attempt to translate or transliterate the Persian word Shāhānshāh. So far it has not been found in any Indian inscription but it is extremely familiar to us from Kuṣāṇa coin-legends from the time of Kāṇiṣka I to that of Vāsudeva I.[5] It is also to be found in a corrupt form on the coins of Vāsudeva II and Kāṇiṣka II.[6] The general tendency of scholars is to take each of the names in the compound *Daivaputra, etc.*, in the Allahabad pillar inscription to denote a separate chief. But the use of the first three titles, Devaputra, Ṣāhi and Ṣāhānuṣāhi indicate that they were used by the Imperial Great Kuṣāṇas only and it is extremely probable that in the time of Samudragupta also they were used by the one and the same prince, the successor of Kāṇiṣka I and Vāsudeva I who ruled over Mathurā and the Panjab. The Śakas may be taken separately to denote the later Western Kṣatrapas of Kathiawad. The Muruṇḍas are certainly a different tribe who are known from literary sources as well as inscription. It is clear therefore from 1.23 of the Allahabad pillar inscrip-

---

1 *Epi. Ind. Vol. XVII, p. 11.*
2 *Ibid. Vol. I, p. 381 ; Vol. IX, p. 240.*
3 *Ibid. Vol. VIII, p. 182.* 4 *Ibid. Vol. IX, p. 242.*
5 *Indian Museum Catalogue, Vol. I, pp. 69–86.* 6 *Ibid, pp. 87–89.*

tion that a descendant of the Imperial Great Kuṣāṇas continued to rule in some parts of North-Western India and was not destroyed by Samudragupta. The full significance of their existence in the 4th century A.D., will be understood when we come to Rāmagupta.

Samudragupta was a great king, perhaps the greatest of his dynasty. He succeeded to a small kingdom but left a large empire to his successor. He reorganised the system of government and administration. He reformed the official system by rejecting the Scythian terms. Henceforth the ranks of officials, their gradations, powers and titles are altogether different. This system continued to be used with slight changes till the final conquest of Northern India by the Musalmans. The bureaucracy was totally unlike that of the Mauryas. He reformed the currency by issuing pure gold coins instead of the base gold of the later Great Kushans and a series of fine copper coins. He struck a new line in numismatics by issuing, if Allan is correct, memorial medals of his father and another relation named Kāca as well as the new type of coins for distributions to Brāhmaṇas, who attended his Aśvamedha ceremony. Like the Imperial and the later Great Kuṣāṇas, Samudragupta did not issue any silver coins.

With the exception of the date in the Gaya copper plate inscription we do not know any other date of this great king. His reign appears to have been very long and very probably he ruled from *circa* 425 to 475 or 480 A.D. We know now that he was succeeded by his son Rāmagupta, though he had selected one of his younger sons, Candragupta as the heir apparent. Samudragupta was very fond of music as Hariṣeṇa has recorded in the Allahabad pillar inscription and as the great king himself has recorded for us in his unique Lyrist coins. We know from the inscriptions that Dattadevī was his queen, perhaps the chief queen (*Agra-Mahiṣī* or *Paṭṭa-Mahādevī*). Like his successors he was also fond of hunting and has commemorated his fondness for tiger huntings in a series of coins. He had not reached regions where the Indian lion was still extant like his second son and grandson.

Rāmagupta, the son and successor of Samudragupta is known to us from a new work on dramaturgy called the *Nāṭyadarpaṇa* by Rāmacandra and Guṇacandra, which mentions and contains fragments of a long-lost historical drama by the celebrated Viśākhadatta, the famous author of *Mudrārākṣasa*. The information was published for the first time by M. Sylvain Levi in a masterly monograph entitled "Deux nouveaux traites de dramaturgie Indienne."[1] From the fragments preserved in the *Nāṭyadarpaṇa* we know that Rāmagupta had become king while Candragupta was still a prince and that the lady Dhruvadevī or Dhruvasvāminī, who later

[1] *Journal Asiatique, Tome CCIII, 1923 pp. 193–218.*

on married Candragupta II and became the mother of the emperor Kumāragupta I and prince Govindagupta, had first married Rāmagupta. This is the earliest instance of a widow marriage among kings of the historical period in Indian history. That Candragupta II had married his brother's widow was definitely remembered even in the 9th century. In the Sanjan plates of Amoghavarṣa I, dated 871 A.D., it is stated "That donor, in the Kali age, who was of the Gupta lineage, having killed (his) brother, we are told, seized (his) kingdom and queen." [1] The extracts from Viśākhadatta's new historical drama *Devī-Candragupta* begin with the second act, where it is stated that Rāmagupta agreed to give away Dhruvadevī to the Śakas in order to remove the apprehensions of his subjects. It appears that the Śaka king had demanded his legally married wife Dhruvadevī of Rāmagupta and that coward had actually consented to send her. The extracts contain a long dialogue between Rāmagupta and Dhruvadevī in which Rāmagupta states that he is sending Dhruvadevi for the sake of the people. [2] Dhruvadevī complains of her husband's heartlessness. Later on Prince Candragupta speaks of the cowardice of her husband, [3] and determines to go to the Śaka king in the guise of Dhruvadevī. [4] Candragupta's

[1] *Verse 48—Epi. Ind., Vol. XVIII, p. 255.*

[2] *Journal Asiatique, Tome CCIII, 1923, p. 203.*

[3] *Ibid., p. 286.* [4] *Ibid., p. 203.*

raid on the Śaka capital and his slaughter of the Śaka king was known to Bāṇa, who says in his *Harṣa-Carita* that Candragupta disguised as a female killed the king of the Śakas, who was desirous of the wife of another, in the city of the enemy.[1] Śaṇkara, the commentator of the *Harṣa-Carita* makes the reference more explicit by stating that the king of the Śakas was killed in private by Candragupta disguised as Dhruvadevī and surrounded by men dressed as women because the former wanted Dhruvadevī, the brother's wife of Candragupta; *Candragupta-bhrātṛjāyām Dhruvadevīm prārthayamānaś=Candraguptena Dhruvadevī-veśadhāriṇā strīveśa-jana-parivṛtena rahasi vyāpāditaḥ.*[2] The subsequent history of Rāmagupta is not known to us from any other source. Evidently after his return to Pāṭaliputra Candragupta succeeded his brother, who was either killed or deposed.[3] The statement of the Sanjan plates of Amoghavarṣa I proves that even in the 9th century, more than two hundred years after Bāṇa, the story of Rāmagupta's deposition and the marriage of his widow with Candragupta II were well remembered. No coins of Rāmagupta have been discovered and it is extremely improbable that he ruled for more than a few months.

---

1 Cowell & Thomas, *Harṣa-carita, Eng. Trans. p. 194.*

2 *Journal Asiatique, Tome CCIII, 1928 pp. 207-8.*

3 The entire available material has been collected and discussed by Prof. A. S. Altekar of the Benares Hindu University—*Journal of the Bihar & Orissa Research Society, Vol. XIV. pp. 223-253.*

Rāmagupta was succeeded by his younger brother Candragupta II, who assumed the title of *Vikramāditya* and is very probably the famous king of that name of Indian folklore. He married his brother's widow Dhruvadevī or Dhruvasvāminī and had by her at least two sons, the emperor Kumāragupta I and Govindagupta. As Kumāragupta succeeded Candragupta II on the throne Druvadevī must have been legally married to her first husband's younger brother. Up to this time the emperors of the Gupta dynasty have been regarded as models of propriety by the most conservative Hindus of the present day. But this instance of widow marriage is bound to shock them. The marriage of Dhruvadevī only strengthens our belief that widow marriages or remarriage, according to the legal principles laid down by Nārada and Parāśara were prohibited later than the 5th century A.D.[1]

Who was this Śaka king, who had suddenly become bold enough to demand of the successor of Samudragupta his legally married wife ? Viśākhadatta calls him a Śaka. In the 19th and 20th centuries we have grown accustomed to identify the later Western Satraps as Śákas in the 3rd and 4th century A.D. But towards the close of the 4th century the power of the Western Satraps had declined very considerably and it is extremely doubtful whether it was possible for any of them to send an open challenge to the Gupta king of

[1] *Nārada, XII, 97 ; Parāśara, IV, 27.*

Pāṭaliputra, the successor of Samudragupta, in the form of a demand for his legally married queen. We know from the Allahabad pillar inscription of Samudragupta that a scion of Kāṇiṣka I was still ruling somewhere in North Western India and it is more probable that it was he who, emboldened by the weakness of Samudragupta's successor, had made this last bold bid for the recovery of the lost Imperial position of his house. It is also more probable that Mathurā was still the capital of the Great Kuṣāṇas and the last great Kuṣāṇa emperor was killed in his palace at Mathurā by Candragupta II disguised as Dhruvadevī and his band of faithful adherents dressed as women.

Candragupta II seems to have spent the first few years after his accession in consolidating his conquest of Mathurā and is the first emperor of the Gupta dynasty whose record has been discovered in that city. His coins, specially his silver coins, are very plentiful all over the Eastern Panjab as far as the banks of the Chenab. There cannot be much doubt about the fact that the final extension of the western frontier of the Gupta empire was due to Candragupta II. His inscriptions prove that he conquered the whole of Mālava and his silver coins indicate that he destroyed the later Western Satraps of Kathiawad. His earliest inscription is a record in a cave near Udaygiri in the Bhilsa district of the Gwalior State, which was excavated in the year 82 by his subordinate, a chief of the Sanakānika tribe with the title of *Mahārāja.* This record proves that practically the whole of North Eastern Mālava had been conquered by Candragupta II before 401-2 A.D. The third inscription comes from Gadhwa in the Allahabad district and adds nothing to our knowledge except a date in the reign of Candragupta II. Two other inscriptions also come from Mālava, only one of which is dated. The Sanchi inscription of the year 93=412-13 A.D., records a donation by Amrakārdava, a dependant of Candragupta II at Kākanādaboṭa. But it supplied us with an important detail that the more familiar name of Candragupta was Devarāja,[1] Another inscription in a cave at Udaygiri near Bhilsa records its excavation by one Vīrasena alias Śāba, who was one of the ministers of Candragupta II. The year 93 of the Sanchi inscriptions is the last known date of Candragupta II. He died and was succeeded by his eldest son Kumāragupta I some time between G. E. 93 and 96 (413—16 A.D.)

From the accession of Candragupta II the Gupta kingdom becomes a vast empire extending from the Kathiawad peninsula to the confines of Eastern Bengal and from the Himalayas to the Narmadā. It is known to have included Bengal, Bihar, United Provinces, Eastern half of the Panjab, portions of the Central Provinces and practically the whole of Central India including the famous and fertile

---

[1] *Gupta Inscriptions pp.* 31-32.

province of Mālava, Northern Gujarat and Kathiawad, including the famous ports of Cambay, Ghogha, Verawal, Porbandar and Dvārakā. The effect of this extension of the Western Frontier was immense on the trade and commerce as well as the culture of Northern India. The European and African trade received immense impulse with the Gupta conquest of the Kathiawad ports. Once more the road from Pāṭaliputra and the great manufacturing cities of Northern and Central India was open right up to the sea. The fine cotton cloths of Eastern Bengal, the silks of Western Bengal, Indigo from Bihar, the golden embroideries and *kinkhwabs* of Benares and Aṇahilapāṭaka or Anhilwāḍā-Pāṭan, the scents and unguents of the hill states of the Himalayas, camphor, sandal and spices from the South were brought to these ports without much interference or the payment of vexatious imposts from each petty chief through whose jurisdiction it passed before the foundation of the Gupta empire. The Western traders poured Roman gold into the country in return for Indian products and the effect of this great wealth on the country is still noticeable in the great variety and number of the coins of Candragupta II. More gold and silver coins of Candragupta II have been discovered than those of his father Samudragupta or his son Kumāragupta I. The most important innovations introduced by Candragupta II were in the currency of the country. He issued gold coins of three different weights. The first of them corresponds to the Kuṣānā standard of 121 grains, the second is of 126 grains and the third of 132 grains. The Kushan standard of 121 grains was an imitation of the standard of the Roman Aureus and Candragupta II appears to have been approaching the ancient Indian Standard of the *Suvarṇa* of 146 grains. To meet the demand of the newly conquered provinces of Gujarat and Kathiawad, Candragupta II issued a new silver coinage. Evidently the gold and copper coinage of Northern India was not acceptable to the local people of Western India, where the silver coinage of the Greek kings Menander and Apollodotos were in circulation even in the first and second century A.D. and where the early and late Western Kṣatrapas issued silver coins only for nearly four hundred years. The silver coinage of Candragupta II was a close copy of that of the Western Kṣatrapas having the king's head and a date in numerals on the obverse with traces of the degenerate Greek legend. The reverse was entirely changed and in the place of the Scythian *Caitya* or *Meru* was placed the celebrated Garuḍa with outspread wings, the family crest or *Lāñchana* of the Imperial Guptas.

Candragupta II allied himself with the only rival power in India of which he was probably afraid, the Vākāṭakas of Central India and the Deccan. By a second queen named Kuberanāgā he had a daughter named Prabhāvatīguptā. This princess was married to the Vākāṭaka king

Rudrasena and had at least two sons, Divākarasena and Pravarasena II. By this alliance Candragupta II protected his left flank and most probably the marriage took place during Candragupta II's campaign in Mālava.

Besides Prabhāvatīguptā, Candragupta II had at least two other issues; Kumāragupta I and Govindagupta. Besides Dhruvadevī the only other known queen of Candragupta II is Kuveranāgā, the mother of the Vākāṭaka queen Prabhāvatīguptā. Candragupta II was also known as Devagupta or Devarāja. This is known in the first place from the Sanchi inscription of the year 93 where Candragupta is specially mentioned as being called Devarāja[1] and in the second place from Vākāṭaka Land Grants in which the father of Prabhāvatīguptā is invariably called Devagupta.[2]

The names of several officers of Candragupta II are known to us from the inscription of his time. The Sanakānīka chief, whose name has been lost in the Udaygiri inscription of the year 82 was evidently an officer of the Gupta empire as he held the rank of a *Mahārāja.* Vīrasena alias Śāba of the undated Udaygiri Cave inscription was another minister (*Anvaya-prāpta-sācivyo*) evidently hereditary.[3] The name of another minister is known to us from the Karamdanda

---

1 *Gupta Inscriptions p. 32.*

2 *Ibid., pp. 237, 246; Epi. Ind. Vol. IX, pp. 267–71.*

3 *Gupta Inscriptions p. 35.*

inscription of the year 117. A Brāhmaṇa named Śikharasvāmin was a second minister of Candragupta II, but held the rank of a *Kumārāmātya.*[1] The only other point worth notice in the reign of Candragupta II is the seal of his queen Dhruvasvāminī, discovered at Basarh, the ancient Vaiśālī. In this seal the queen calls herself "The Great Queen, the illustrious Dhruvasvāminī, the wife of the Mahārājādhirāja, the illustrious Candragupta, the mother of the Mahārāja, the illustrious Govindagupta."[2] It is impossible to understand now why the great queen calls herself the mother of Govindagupta only and not that of her eldest son the emperor Kumāragupta I. She is acknowledged as the mother of Kumāragupta I in the Bilsad pillar inscription of the year 96,[3] and the official seal of the infant emperor Kumāragupta II[4] as well as the semi-official inscription on the pillars at Bihar[5] and Kahaon.[6]

The Chinese pilgrim Fa Hsien visited India during the reign of Candragupta II. The Chinese monk has forgotten even to name the ruling emperor though he describes Pāṭaliputra, the Imperial capital, as one of the most flourishing cities. Gaya and the neighbouring district, the Mecca of Buddhism, was covered with jungle.

---

1 *Epi. Ind. Vol. X, p. 71.*

2 *Annual Report of the Archæological Survey of India 1903-4, p. 107, pl. XL. 1.*

3 *Gupta Inscriptions p. 43.*

4 *J.A.S.B., 1889, Part. I, pp. 89.*

5 *Gupta Inscriptions, p. 50.*

6 *Ibid., p. 53.*

We can obtain tolerably reliable information about the condition of Northern India at the beginning of the 6th century A.D. from Fa Hsien's travels.

Candragupta II, the third emperor of the dynasty, raised the kingdom left by his father to the status of an empire. He became the virtual master of Northern India by destroying the Scythians of the Panjab and Western India. He was unquestionably the paramount sovereign of India at the time of his death. By the marriage alliance with the Vākāṭakas he had neutralised the only rival power in India. Like all great kings he was totally unscrupulous, which is proved by his deposition or murder of his eldest brother Rāmagupta. Like Akbar and Śivājī he was brave to the point of rashness, which is proved by his adventure in disguise with a chosen band of followers in the city or camp of the Scythian kings. He was an ambitious man and a good general and therefore succeeded in annexing the Eastern Panjab, Mālava, Gujarat and Kathiawad to his inherited dominions. He also issued a varied gold coinage like his father. The most significant type of his gold coins is the Lion-slayer type which perhaps indicates his lion hunting either in the deserts of Rajputana or in Kathiawad.

Kumāragupta I, the son and successor of Candragupta II, began his reign peacefully, but it ended in disaster. The earlier part of his long reign of over 40 years was by far the most prosperous period in the total rule of the Gupta dynasty. The impetus received by the Western overseas trade and the influx of foreign gold into the country manifested itself in a great revival of art. It was in this reign that Gupta Architecture and Sculpture received its final form. The influence of art is also to be distinctly seen in the coins of the ruling emperor, which are the finest of the entire series.

At some period between 414 and 455, A.D. the Gupta empire was invaded by horde after horde of barbarians who succeeded in destroying it and its culture after three quarters of a century. The earliest invasion of the barbarians was successfully dispelled by the Crown Prince, Skandagupta, but later on the strain of continual warfare was felt by the Treasury and the emperor was compelled to issue coins of impure gold. Though a number of inscriptions of the reign of Kumāragupta I have been discovered, the chronology of the wars with the barbarians is imperfectly known to us. The undated Gaḍhwā inscription records the gift of ten gold coins (*Dīnāras*) for an alms house. [1] Another from the same place records the erection of a house for the free distribution of food.[2] The Bilsad pillar inscription records the erection of a gateway, another house for the free distribution of food as well as gifts to a temple of Kārtikeya in the year 96. [3] An image of a Jaina Tīrthaṅkara was dedi-

[1] *Gupta Inscriptions*, p. 40. [2] *Ibid.* p. 41. [3] *Ibid.* pp. 43-44.

cated at Mathurā in the year **113**. In same year a grant or transfer of land was recorded on a copper plate in Bengal. This plate has been recovered in a fragmentary condition and nothing can be recovered beyond the name of the reigning sovereign, the date and the name of the *Viṣaya*, which is read as Khusā-pāra by me [1] and Khaḍā-pāra by Prof. Radhagovinda Basak. [2] The copper plates discovered in recent years at Damodarpur in the Dinajpur district of Bengal are far more illuminating. Out of five plates discovered at Damodarpur two belong to the reign of Kumāragupta I; plate No. I dated G.E. 124, and plate No. II dated G.E. 128. The first plate records that in G.E. 124 when the *Paramadaivata-Paramabhaṭṭāraka-Mahārājādhirāja* Kumāragupta was the ruling emperor, an *Uparika* named Ciratadatta was the governor of Puṇḍravardhana-*Bhukti* (Division). Under him the *Kumārāmātya* Vetravarman was the deputy governor of the district of Koṭivarṣa. It records further that a Brāhmaṇa of the name of Karppaṭika applied to the local officials for the sale of a piece of waste land to him. The application was sanctioned and the sale confirmed by the inscription on the plate. [3] The second plate from Damodarpur belonging to the reign of Kumāragupta I records that in G.E. 128 the *Uparika* Cirātadatta was still the governor of

---

[1] *P. & J.A.S. B., Vol. V. 1909, pp. 459-61.*

[2] *Epi. Ind., Vol. XVII, p. 347.*

[3] *Ibid. Vol. XV, pp. 130-31.*

the *Bhukti* of Puṇḍravardhana and the *Kumārāmātya* Vetravarman, the deputy governor of the district of Koṭivarṣa. In that year another person applied for a transfer of waste land to him at the usual price for the maintenance of the five *Mahāyajñas.* The application was sanctioned and the transfer recorded on the plate.[1] The next record of the reign of Kumāragupta I is Buddhist. An image of Buddha was dedicated in G. E.129 by a Buddhist monk named Buddhamitra. The image was discovered in the Karchhana *Tahsil* of the Allahabad district and the only noticeable point in this record is the title of *Mahāraja* given to Kumāragupta I, instead of the current form of Mahārājādhirāja.[2] It should be noticed in this connection that the small Jaina votive inscription from Mathura uses both *Paramabhaṭṭāraka* and *Mahārājādhirāja.*[3] We possess no records of the last seven years of this emperor's reign. It was most probably during this period the Hūṇa wars mentioned in the inscriptions of Skandagupta took place. We know from the silver coins that Kumāragupta I reigned till G.E. 136=455-6 A.D.,[4] and that his eldest son Skandagupta was on the throne in the same year.

The long reign of Kumāragupta I brought the prosperous part of the Gupta period to an end. With the accession of Skandagupta begins the

---

[1] *Ibid. pp. 133-34.* [2] *Gupta Inscriptions, pp. 46-47.*

[3] *Epi. Ind., Vol. II, p. 210, No. XXXIX.*

[4] *J.A.S.B. Vol. LXIII, 1894, Part I, p. 175.*

next dark period of Indian history, which ends only with the rise of the Rajputs in the 7th and 8th centuries, save and except for the well illuminated reign of Harṣavardhana in the first half of the 7th century. Skandagupta was most probably the eldest son of Kumāragupta I. We know the name of only one queen of Kumāragupta I named Anantadevī, who was the mother of Puragupta, the successor of Skandagupta. Among the officers of the reign of Kumāragupta I we know only one other person besides the *Uparika* Cirātadatta of Puṇḍravardhana or Northern Bengal and his subordinate the *Kumārāmātya* Vetravarman. This is Pṛthivīṣeṇa, the son of Candragupta II's minister Śikharasvāmin. Pṛthivīṣeṇa was at first a *Kumārāmātya* and a minister (*Mantrin*), but later on he became the Commander-in-chief (*Mahābalādhikṛta*).[1] Of the inscriptions of the reign of Skandagupta which indicate very clearly that the closing years of the reign of Kumāragupta I were not passed in peace, we have referred to before.

Kumāragupta I, the fourth emperor of the Gupta dynasty, cannot be compared to his father and grandfather. He was probably weak in character and fond of a life of easy indolence. In the absence of official inscriptions of his reign, like the Allahabad pillar inscription of Samudragupta or the Bhitari pillar inscription of Skanda-

---

[1] *Epi. Ind. Vol. X., p. 72.*

gupta, it is extremely difficult to assert anything with certainty. But the general trend of events of his reign and the subsequent disruption of the Gupta empire in the time of his second son, Puragupta, indicates that he was no intrepid leader of men like his grandfather or a notable general like his father. He assumed the title of *Mahendrāditya* in imitation of his father's *biruda Vikramāditya*. His coinage is more varied than that of his father. He introduced many new types in the gold coinage, the most notable among which are his very rare Aśvamedha coins. These coins alone prove that like his grandfather Samudragupta, Kumāragupta I also had performed the Aśvamedha ceremony. He issued two different types of gold coins reminiscent of his hunting exploits. Like his grandfather Samudragupta he issued one type representing him as killing a tiger and like his father Candragupta II he issued another type of coins representing him as killing a lion. His name Kumāra is synonymous with that of the divine general Kārtikeya and according to the laudations of the court-poets he compared himself with that god and issued a new type of gold coins accordingly. On this type we see the king feeding a peacock on the obverse and the god Kārtikeya riding on a peacock on the reverse. He issued a new type of silver coins for use in Central India in which Garuḍa, the family symbol is replaced by the peacock. Later on this type was copied by Śilāditya and

Harṣavardhana. He continued the issue of silver coins of the Western Kṣatrapa type initiated by his father but was compelled in times of stress, during the first Hūṇa war to mint this type on silver-plated copper instead of pure silver.

Of our progenitors, whom we ought to have remembered with gratitude, but whom centuries of Musalman oppression, rapine, and destruction of records have caused us to forget, the emperor Skandagupta stands in the foremost rank. When the great Magadhan nation forgot its glorious past, its sacred duty of defending the gods and Brāhmaṇas, women and children, the weak and the helpless and above all the defence of the mother-land, he alone remembered it, tried his best to maintain the glorious record of his ancestors from being tarnished and the rich and fertile plains of the Indus and Ganges from being trampled under the feet of countless hordes of barbarian Huns. He was the last great hero of Magadha who realised that it was his duty to defend the gates of India with the last drop of his life blood. He spent his whole life in the performance of this noble task and at the end of it sacrificed himself cheerfully in the performance of this sacred duty.

We possess a number of records of Skandagupta's reign from which the chronology can be reconstructed very accurately but the most important among them is the undated official inscription on the pillar at Bhitari in the Ghazipur district. The earliest record in the chronological order is the great Junagadh rock inscription of his governor of Kathiawad, Parṇadatta and his son Cakrapālita. This record contains three different dates, 136, 137, and 138, all in the Gupta era and must be read jointly with the Junagadh rock inscription of the Mahākṣatrapa Rudradāman I of 150 A.D. We learn from this inscription that the Vaiṣya Viceroy Puṣyagupta of the emperor Candragupta of the Maurya dynasty had caused a great lake named Sudarśana to be constructed at the foot of the mount Girnar or Urjayanta near Raivataka and that the Yavana king Tuṣāspha, the Viceroy of the great Maurya emperor Aśoka had excavated irrigation canals from this great lake. During the reign of Rudradāman I, in the Śaka year 72=150 A.D., this great lake burst through its bonds on account of excessive rain. The dams were rebuilt by Suviśākha, son of Kulaipa, a Pahlava, the minister of Rudradāman I.[1] This great lake, the Sudarśana, once more burst its bunds on the night of the 6th day of Prauṣṭhapada (August-September) of G.E. 136 (455-56 A.D.) and was repaired by the orders of the emperor Skandagupta when Parṇadatta was the Viceroy of Surāṣṭra or Kathiawad under the superintendence of the latter's son Cakrapālita. The new dam was of masonry and on it Cakrapalita built a temple of Viṣṇu in G.E. 138=457-58 A.D. The bed of the ancient Sudar-

[1] *Epi. Ind. Vol. VIII. pp. 42–49.*

śana lake is now a fertile plain surrounding the base of Mount Girnar near the city of Junagadh in the state of that name in Kathiawad. The inscriptions of Rudradāman I and Skandagupta are to be found on the same boulder on which the great Aśoka had caused his fourteen rock edicts to be inscribed for the information of the people of Surāṣṭra. No trace can be found of the great embankments or the temple of Viṣṇu built by Cakrapālita.

Most of the historical information about Skandagupta and the Hūṇa wars is to be derived from his Bhitari pillar inscription. Bhitari is the name of a village about five miles to the north-east of Saiyadpur, a village and the headquarters of a *tahsil* in the Ghazipur district. A red sand stone pillar stands outside the village and bears on it a long inscription in 19 lines for the most part in a very good state of preservation. It is from this inscription that we learn that Skandagupta spent a whole night on the bare ground during the Hūṇa wars in his father's life time in his attempts to restore the fallen fortunes of his family. "By whom, when he prepared himself to restore the fallen fortunes of (*his*) family, a (*whole*) night was spent on a couch that was the bare earth; and then having conquered the Pushyamitras, who had developed great power and wealth, he placed (*his*) left foot on a foot-stool which was the king (*of that tribe himself*).[1] Some doubts

[1] *Gupta Inscriptions pp. 53-54, 55.*

have been expressed about the reading of the name Puṣyamitra and it has been suggested that this should be read as *Ayudhya-mitrāṃś=ca* but a close examination of the original shows that the suggested reading is impossible on account of the impossibility of the second syllable being *yu*.

Of the events connected with the Hūṇa war the same inscription informs us that "Who, when (*his*) father had attained the skies, conquered (*his*) enemies by the strength of (*his*) arm, and established again the ruined fortunes of (*his*) lineage; and then crying 'The victory has been achieved,' betook himself to (*his*) mother, whose eyes were full of tears from joy, just as Kṛishṇa, when he had slain (*his*) enemies, betook himself to (*his mother*) Devakī;

"Who, with his own armies, established (*again his*) lineage that had been made to totter ...., (*and*) with his two arms subjugated the earth, (*and*) shewed mercy to the conquered people in distress, (*but*) has become neither proud nor arrogant though his glory is increasing day by day; (*and*) whom the bards raised to distinction with (*their*) songs and praises;

"By whose two arms the earth was shaken, when he, the creator (*of a disturbance like that*) of a terrible whirlpool, joined in close conflict with the Hūṇas;"[1]

The Bhitari pillar inscription proves that as the

[1] *Ibid.*, pp. 55-56.

Crown Prince Skandagupta had saved his father's kingdom from total destruction at the hands of the Puṣyamitras, who were probably the first wave of the Hūṇas to reach the plains of the Panjab. It also proves that after his accession as emperor he had defeated the second wave of the Hūṇas and thus saved Northern India from the ravages of a barbarian invasion. His defeat of the Hūṇas is not referred in any other inscription of his reign.

The Hūṇas are known to the western historians as the Huns and to the Chinese as the Hiung Nu. We hear of them for the first time in connection with the Yueh Chi or the Kuṣāṇas in the history of the First Han dynasty. The subsequent history and the migrations of these people have been very closely followed by French scholars. The researches of Messieurs Chavannnes and Berthoud have proved conclusively that the Huns spread over Southern Asia and Europe like swarms of locusts towards the close of the 5th century A.D. While Attila terrified the Roman emperors of the east and the west, Khiṅkhila and Toramāṇa devastated the fairest provinces of Persia and India. The Eastern branch of the Hūṇa tribes are known to European writers as the Epthalites while the Chinese call them Ye-tha. Two successive kings of Persia were killed in battle with the Hūṇas. Western writers describe them as a nomadic people with Mongolian features. The affinities between the Hungarian or the Magyar language and the Tibetan proves that some of the Western Tibetan tribes are the modern representatives of the Hūṇas. This is borne out by the fact that the country to the north of the Māna-sarovar lake and the Nīlam pass is still known to the people of the Garhwal State as the *Hūṇa-deśa*.

In India, we do not know what preparations were made by the emperor Kumāragupta I and Skandagupta to meet this outburst of barbarians through the Northern passes. The Hūṇa kings Toramāṇa and Mihirakula are accredited with the destruction of the ancient Buddhist temples and establishments of the North Western Frontier Province, the ancient Gandhāra, Udyāna and Uraśa. Pāṭaliputra was still the capital of India and Magadha still the leader of the nations of Northern India. Did the Magadhans realise the importance of the sacred trust placed in their charge by the people of Northern India? The verdict of history is against them. For the last time in the history of Magadha the people of that province failed in their duty. The Western gate of India was neglected in the time of Kumāragupta I and swarm after swarm of barbarians poured through it. Chinese historians have recorded the destruction of the cities of Bactria and Afghanistan. Did Kumāragupta I make any attempt to succour the minor Kuṣāṇa chiefs of these two countries? Our records are silent on this point and we have to admit that at the supreme moment the people of Magadha belied their trust. The horrors of a barbarian invasion and a long war in a country far away from the fertile plains of the Indus and the Ganges, full of bleak and arid mountains, for the most part of the year covered with eternal snow, did not appeal to the sons of Magadha in the fifth century A.D. The influx of Roman gold and the soft life of a century of peace and prosperity had enervated the people of Magadha. Consequently the great passes of the North West were not defended and the fertile valleys of Kapiśa, Nagarahāra and Gandhāra were wiped out, as it were, from the map of India of the 5th century A.D. After the lapse of fifteen centuries we can only imagine the plight of the helpless population at the mercy of the merciless uncouth unwashen barbarians. City after city went up in flames, the male population lay massacred on their door-steps and the women and children dragged away into slavery. Thus perished the last vestiges of the great civilisation of the Asiatic Greeks in India, which had absorbed the Śaka, the Kuṣāṇa and other barbarian invaders of the country. With it perished the noblest monuments of the great Kuṣāṇa emperors, their temples and monasteries and rich endowments. At the same time perished the great University of Taxila, for centuries the greatest centre of learning in the country.

Skandagupta warded off the first blow during the life time of his father. The second blow also he parried with difficulty. The strain on the treasury was enormous and the emperor was compelled to debase the gold coinage like his father. The subsequent history of the reign of Skandagupta is not known to us. But the Hūṇa invasions continued and most probably Skandagupta lost his life in trying to stem the mighty flood of the third invasion. We know from the Kahaum inscription that Skandagupta was alive in 141 G.E. when a man named Madra dedicated five images of the *Ādikartṛs* or *Tīrthaṅkaras* on a stone column in the village of Kakubha in the modern *tahsil* of Deoriya in the Gorakhpur district.[1] Silver coins were issued by Skandagupta in G.E. 145. In G.E. 146, when Śarvanāga was the deputy governor (*Viṣayapati*) of the *Antarvedī* or the country between the Ganges and the Jumna a Brāhmaṇa named Devaviṣṇu gave some land for the maintenance of a lamp in a temple of the Sun in the town of Indrapura (perhaps the same as Indor Khera in the Anupshahr *tahsil* of the Bulandshahr district) built by the Kṣatriyas Achalavarman and Bhrukuṇṭhasiṁha at the same place.[2] The latest known date of the emperor Skandagupta is the year G.E. 148=467-8 A.D., to be found on certain silver coins.[3]

With the discovery of two new inscriptions in the ancient province of Mālava a new problem has arisen in connection with the period of warfare which followed the death of Kumāragupta I.

---

1 *Gupta Inscriptions pp. 66-7.*

2 *Ibid., pp. 70-71.*

3 *J.R.A.S., 1889, p. 134.*

The first of these two is the Tumain inscription of G.E., 116=435-36 A.D. In this record Govindagupta is mentioned once and then follows the name of another person named Ghaṭotkacagupta. From other Gupta inscriptions we know that Ghaṭotkacagupta was the name of the father of Candragupta I. From the Poona plates of the Vākāṭaka queen Prabhāvatīguptā the same information is to be derived.[1] Mr. M. B. Garde, Superintendent Archaeology in the Gwalior State has published a short note on the Tumain inscription of G.E. 116 but in this note the exact relationship between Govindagupta and Ghaṭotkacagupta has not been made clear. The inscription has not been published in full.[2] To the same scholar belongs the credit of another important inscription at Mandasor in the Malwa *Prant* of the Gwalior State. This inscription mentions Govindagupta immediately after Candragupta II and is dated V.S. 524. Therefore it must be admitted that Govindagupta was alive in V.S. 524=467-8 A.D., which is the last known date of the emperor Skandagupta.[3] Now the problem is about Govindagupta's position in Mālava. Was he the Viceroy of Mālava in G.E. 116=435-36 A.D., or had he thrown off the allegiance of his

1 *Epi. Ind. Vol. XV, p. 41.*

2 *Ind. Ant. Vol. XLIX, pp. 114-5.*

3 I am indebted to Mr. M. B. Garde for permission to use this information from the newly discovered inscription from Mandasor.

brother? The second inscription shows that in 467-8 A.D., he was still in Mālava. But the second inscription does not mention Skandagupta. Did Govindagupta refuse to acknowledge his nephew after his brother's death in 455 A.D., or had he done so after Skandagupta's death? These problems will remain unsolved till fresh material about the later history of Mālava is available.

A period of anarchy and misrule begins with the death of Skandagupta. He was succeeded on the throne by his younger brother, probably a step-brother, Puragupta. Puragupta is known to be the son of Anantadevī who was not the mother of Skandagupta and Skandagupta's mother is deliberately omitted in all official genealogies of the Gupta dynasty. The name of Skandagupta is also omitted from the geneology in the official seal of Puragupta's grandson Kumāragupta II discovered at Bhitari in the Ghazipur district. In many other cases where a brother succeeds instead of a son the names of both brothers are mentioned if relations are cordial. The best known examples are the Banskhera[1] and Madhuban[2] plates of Harṣavardhana and the Manahali plate of Madanapāla[3] of Bengal. Even if we compare a seal with a seal and place the Sonpat seal of Harṣavardhana by the side of the Bhitari seal of Kumā-

---

[1] *Epi. Ind. Vol. IV, pp. 210-11.*

[2] *Ibid., Vol. I, pp. 72-73. Vol. VII, pp. 157-8.*

[3] *J.A.S.B., Vol. LXIX, 1900, Part I. pp. 93ff.*

ragupta II then we are forced to admit that the name of Skandagupta was intentionally omitted from the latter. The find-spots of coins of the three later Gupta emperors, Puragupta, Narasiṁhagupta and Kumāragupta II indicate very definitely that these three monarchs had very little authority outside Bengal, Bihar and the Eastern districts of United Provinces; such as Mirzapur and Basti. From these facts we can glean that the Imperial authority was limited to the metropolitan districts of the Gupta empire and that Puragupta was not on good terms with his elder brother and predecessor Skandagupta. It would be natural to surmise that during the third Hūṇa war Puragupta had set himself up as a rival emperor in Magadha and thus became the cause of Skandagupta's defeat and death. It is this treachery on the part of his younger nephew which seems to have made Govindagupta disobedient in Mālava.

Evidently the revenues of the empire had diminished severely on account of the defection of the western provinces. None of these three emperors issued any silver coins, proving thereby that Central India, Gujarat and Kathiawad had ceased to obey them. The precarious condition of the Imperial finances compelled Puragupta to issue coins of base gold. His coins are extremely rare; there being two coins in the immense collection of the British Museum. Allan is inclined to assign the Horseman-type issues of Prakāśāditya to Puragupta, but there is no evidence in his favour. It is therefore more probable that Puragupta's reign lasted for a few months only. The recent discoveries of dated inscriptions of the time of Kumāragupta II and Budhagupta at Sarnath prove that three generations of Gupta emperors have to be crowded into the short period of six years. Skandagupta, the grand-uncle of Kumāragupta II was ruling in 467-8 A.D., and we learn from the Sarnath inscriptions that Kumāragupta II was recognised as the ruling sovereign in G.E. 154=473-74 A.D.[1] Out of these six years the greatest portion has to be assigned to Narasiṁhagupta, the son and successor of Puragupta because a larger number of his gold coins have been discovered in comparison with his father Puragupta. It would be perfectly fair, therefore, to assume that Puragupta's reign came to an end in 468 or at the latest in 469 A.D., and he was succeeded by his son Narasiṁhagupta. Puragupta assumed the *biruda* of *Vikrama* and most probably the complete form was *Vikramāditya*, like that of his grandfather Candragupta II. Narasiṁhagupta is known to us, like his father Puragupta and his son Kumāragupta II from his coins only. They are to be found in larger number in Bengal proper than in Bihar or in the United Provinces. Twelve of them are preserved in the British Museum and

[1] *Annual Report of the Arch. Survey of India, 1914-15, part II, pp. 124-25.*

only six in the Indian Museum in Calcutta. A reign of four years would therefore be quite sufficient for him. The more so because we know now that his son and successor Kumāragupta II was on the throne in 473-74 A.D. Narasiṁhagupta assumed the *biruda* of *Bālāditya*, a title which has caused much misunderstanding among scholars.

Kumāragupta II must have been an infant in arms when he was placed on the throne. Though his great-grandfather Kumāragupta I had reigned for 41 years, his grandfather Puragupta must have died about 468-69 A.D., and therefore Narasiṁhagupta must have come to the throne while very young and consequently his son Kumāragupta II must have been an infant. There are parallels of this type in the history of India. Aurangzeb 'Alamgīr ascended the throne in 1556 and died after a reign of 51 years in 1707. His son S̲h̲āh 'Alam I Bahādur ascended the throne at a very advanced age in 1707 and lived to rule for 5 years only. S̲h̲āh 'Alam's eldest son Mui'zzuddīn Jahāndār S̲h̲āh had passed the prime of his life when he ascended the throne in 1712 and was murdered in the next year. Jahāndār's nephew Farrūk̲h̲siyar was very young when he ascended the throne and the sons of his younger uncles Jahān S̲h̲āh and Rafia'-us̲h̲-s̲h̲ān were still young at that time. There is therefore no reason to be surprised at the fact that Kumārgupta II in the fourth generation after Kumāragupta I was an infant in arms. He assumed the *biruda* of *Kramāditya* in imitation of the *Vikramāditya* of his grandfather Puragupta and his great-great-grandfather Candragupta II. There are eighteen of his gold coins in the British Museum and only two in the Indian Museum, Calcutta, which is not strange in consideration of the fact that his short rule was over before G.E. 157=476-77 A.D. This is proved by the Sarnath inscription of the time of Budhagupta.

The chronology of the later Imperial Guptas has received much attention from scholars since the discovery of the Sarnath inscriptions of the time of Kumāragupta II and Budhagupta. After the discovery of the Bhitari seal of Kumāragupta II, the late Dr. V. A. Smith had propounded the theory that Skandagupta ruled till 480 A.D., and Kumaragupta II till 530 A.D.[1] Subsequently he was of opinion that Puragupta came to the throne in 468 and Narasiṁhagupta shortly afterwards. He placed the accession of Kumāragupta II in 473 and Budhagupta in 476 A.D.,[2] according to the views of the writer[3] and Dr. R. C. Majumdar.[4] Inspite of these discussions a number of writers still continue to believe that "The genealogy of the imperial Guptas continued

1 *Early History of India, 3rd Edition p. 327.*

2 *Ibid., 4th Edition, p. 346.*

3 *Annals of the Bhandarkar Institute, Vol. I, 1919, part I, pp. 67-80.*

4 *P. and J.A.S.B., Vol. XVII, 1921, pp. 249-55; Ind. Ant. Vol. XLVII, 1918, pp. 166-7.*

through Skandagupta for a period of still about three quarters of a century, and that the Gupta empire did not perish after the death of Skandagupta, as had long been held by historians."[1] It is absolutely useless to discuss incoherent theories of writers who would believe inspite of total want of evidence that the Kumāragupta who is mentioned in the Sarnath image inscription of G.E. 154 was Kumāragupta II and the son of Skandagupta and that Budhagupta was the son and successor of this Kumāragupta. Further Puragupta, Narasiṁhagupta and Kumāragupta are taken to belong to a different branch altogether. Whatever may be the case there is no evidence to prove that Kumāragupta II was a son of Skandagupta and that Budhagupta was the son of this Kumāragupta II. There is no evidence in favour of the existence of a third Kumāragupta in addition to the sons of Candragupta II and Narasiṁhagupta. Writers of this class depend upon untenable theories of older writers. Because Drs. V. A. Smith and Hoernle had hazarded the proposition that a Kumāragupta ruled in 530 A.D., therefore there must be a Kumāragupta at that date. The bases of Hoernle and Smith's theories of the dates of Skandagupta and Kumāragupta II are the statements of the Yuan Chwang about the defeat of the Hūṇa king Mihirakula by a confederacy of kings under the leadership of

---

1 *Epi. Ind., Vol. XV, p. 119.*

a king named Bālāditya. Identifying this king with Narasiṁhagupta Fleet and Hoernle placed Skandagupta's death in 480 A.D., and Kumāragupta II in 530 A.D. The discovery of the Sarnath and Damodarpur inscriptions makes it unnecessary to discuss this point any further.

We do not know how the infant king Kumāragupta II came to lose the throne or died. Budhagupta's relationship with Skandagupta or Puragupta is also unknown to us. There cannot be any doubt about the fact that Budhagupta succeeded Kumāragupta II because the former's earliest date, the Sarnath inscription of G.E. 157=476-77 A.D., is only three years removed from the only known date of Kumāragupta II, the Sarnath inscription of G.E. 154=473-74 A.D. Budhagupta is taken by some scholars to be a son of Kumāragupta I because the latter's *biruda Mahendra* is equivalent to *Śakra* in Sanskrit and according to Yuan Chwang Budhagupta's father's name was *Śakrāditya*. The principal difficulties about the chronology of events of the reign of Budhagupta are the want of any official stone inscription like the Allahabad pillar inscription of Samudragupta or the Bhitari pillar inscription of Skandagupta and the want of any gold coins bearing his name. It is quite possible that the coins bearing the *biruda Prakāśāditya* were issued by him, but his name Budhagupta has not been found on any of them. Budhagupta succeeded in re-uniting the whole of the Gupta empire.

Two of his inscriptions have been discovered at Sarnath, near Benares, but they are of no historical interest as they record dedications of images of Buddha by a Buddhist monk. The Damodarpur plates contain two transfers of land which took place in his reign. From the inscription on the first of these plates we learn that during the reign of Budhagupta the *Uparika* Brahmadatta, with the title of *Mahārāja*, was the Viceroy of the division (*bhukti*) of Puṇḍravardhana. A villager named Nābhaka applied for the sale of some land, free of revenue, for the settlement of some Brāhmaṇas and the sale was recorded in this inscription. At the time of the issue of the second plate the *Uparika Mahārāja* Jayadatta was the Viceroy of the division of Puṇḍravardhana and under him an *Āyuktaka* was the governor of a district (*viṣaya*) of Koṭivarṣa. At this time the *Nagara-Śreṣṭhin*[1] Ṛbhupāla applied for some land, probably unsettled (*apradā*) land, on the Himalayas in the village of Doṅgāgrāma for the purpose of building two temples to the gods Kokāmukha-svāmin and Śveta-Varāha-svāmin and for the establishment of one *Nāmaliṅgam* and according to this application some homestead (*vāstu*) land was sold to him and a transfer recorded on this plate.[2] In G.E., 165=484-85 A.D., Budhagupta was recognised as

[1] This office corresponded to the modern *Nagarseṭhs* of Gujarat. There is a *Nagarseṭh* in Ahmadabad even now.

[2] *Epi. Ind.*, Vol. *XV*, *pp. 137–41.*

the sovereign of Mālava. In that year a Viceroy named Suraśmicandra was ruling the country between the Jumna (*Yamunā*) and the Narmadā. In that year a Brāhmaṇa named Mātṛviṣṇu, who held the title of Mahārāja and his brother Dhanyaviṣṇu, who were the great-grandsons of the Ṛṣi Indraviṣṇu, grandsons of Varuṇaviṣṇu and sons of Hariviṣṇu erected a flag-staff (*dhvaja-stambha*) of the god Janārdana.[1] This inscription is a very important record for later imperial Gupta chronology as it enables us to determine the approximate date of the Hūṇa conquest of Mālava. Budhagupta issued a silver coinage of the Central Indian type but these coins also are very rare. The British Museum contains only three specimens and one of these three bear the latest date of this monarch, G.E. 175=494-95 A.D.

We do not know who succeeded Budhagupta. But in G.E. 224=543-44 A.D., a king named Bhānugupta was acknowledged as the emperor in Northern Bengal. An inscription on a pillar discovered at Eran mentions the same Bhānugupta. In G.E. 191=510-11 A.D., the king Bhānugupta came to Eran with a subordinate chief named Goparāja and fought a great battle in which Goparāja was killed. The latter's wife mounted the funeral pyre and evidently the pillar was erected on that spot. A comparison of the Eran pillar

[1] *Gupta Inscriptions*, pp. 88-90.

inscription of G.E. 165, the pillar inscription of G.E. 191 and that on the great image of the Boar incarnation dedicated at the same place in the first year of the Hūṇa king Toramāṇa enables us to deduce the date of the conquest of Northern Mālava by the Hūṇa king Toramāṇa. It has been noted above that in the Eran pillar inscription of G.E. 165, the brothers Mātṛviṣṇu and Dhanyaviṣṇu erected a flag-staff of Janārdana. It has also been noted that a great battle was fought at Eran by an emperor named Bhānugupta in G.E., 191.[1] We find that Dhanyaviṣṇu alone, after the decease of his elder brother Mātṛviṣṇu, erected a temple of the Boar incarnation of Viṣṇu. This inscription is incised on the breast of colossal image of the Varāha incarnation of Viṣṇu. The temple and the image are still lying at Eran.[2] From these three inscriptions we can deduce the following facts:—

1. That the conquest of Mālava took place within one generation of the dedication of the flag-staff of Viṣṇu by the brothers Mātṛviṣṇu and Dhanyaviṣṇu.
2. That the battle of Eran, in which Goparāja was killed, was fought by Bhānugupta with the Hūṇas and that he was defeated.
3. That Toramāṇa was the Hūṇa king who conquered Mālava and defeated Bhānugupta.

---

1 *Ibid.*, *pp.* 91–93. 2 *Ibid.*, *pp.* 158–61.

Bhānugupta was still living in G.E., 224=543-44 A.D., when he was recognised as the ruling emperor in Northern Bengal. In that year a person of the royal family whose name was Rājaputradeva was the Viceroy of the division of Puṇḍravardhana and under him Svayambhudeva was the governor of the district of Kotivarṣa. At that time the *Nagaraśreṣṭhin* Ṛbhupāla was also living. In that year an application was made by one Amṛtadeva, an inhabitant of Ayodhyā, for the purchase of some rent-free land, at the usual price, for the provision of repairs to the temple of Śveta-Varāha-svāmin in the forest and for the perpetuation of certain supplies to the same temple. According to this application a certain amount of homestead and cultivable land was transferred to the god Śveta-Varāha-svāmin as a perpetual endowment. This plate bears the seal of the office of the head quarters of Koṭivarṣa.[1] This is the last known record of Bhānugupta, none of whose coins have been discovered up to date.

We know that a number of minor kings succeeded Budhagupta and Bhānugupta in North-Eastern India. They are known solely from their coins discovered in Bengal. The oldest of these coins belong to Candragupta III, *Dvādaśāditya* which were discovered at Kalighat near Calcutta during the *regime* of Warren Hastings as Governor of the Presidency of Bengal and were sent to Eng-

[1] *Epi. Ind., Vol. XVIII, pp. 141–44.*

land. The next king was Viṣṇugupta *Candrāditya*. The British Museum possesses three coins of Candragupta III and fifteen coins of Viṣṇugupta, most of which came from the Kalighat hoard. The Indian Museum at Calcutta possesses only two coins of Viṣṇugupta. The coins of Jayagupta *Prakāṇḍayaśā* belong to a later period, apparently the end of the 6th century A.D. During the rule of these *rois faineants* the distant provinces of the Gupta empire gradually became independent. A general named Bhaṭakka or Bhaṭārka became practically independent in Kathiawad in Gujarat and was able to make the governorship hereditary. He was succeeded in turn by four of his sons named Dharasena I, Droṇasiṁha, Dhruvasena and Dharapaṭṭa. Bhaṭārka and his eldest son Dharasena I were content with the modest title of *Senāpati*, but the remaining three sons assumed the title of Maharaja. Assumption of the Imperial right of issuing grants of land was assumed by the sons of Bhaṭarka from 502 or 526 A.D. This shows that Kathiawad remained loyal during the life time of Budhagupta but the mask of loyalty was cast aside early in the reign of Bhānugupta and even in the life time of that emperor, Dhruvasena I and his successor openly issued grants of land without even mentioning the name of the reigning emperor. A comparison with the grants issued by royal officers of the Imperial Guptas such as the Indor plate of the reign of Skandagupta of G.E., 146 or the Damodarpur plates of the time of Budhagupta at once proves the difference in the attitude. In the Indore plate the Viceroy Śarvanāga of the country between the Ganges and the Jumna mentions the emperor Skandagupta explicitly. So also in the Damodarpur plates the Viceroy of Puṇḍravardhana mentions the emperor Budhagupta. We find a complete change in the Bhamodra Mohota plates of Mahārāja Droṇasiṁha, who ushers himself simply by the phrase "Who meditated on the feet of the Great king of kings." The Bhamodra Mohota plates were issued after the last known date of Budhagupta and before the earliest known date of Bhānugupta.[1]

The imperial prerogative of issuing grants of land was also usurped by another family of feudatories. Hastin ruled over the country between Allahabad and Maihar and started issuing grants of land in his own name during the life time of Budhagupta. The earliest charter issued by this prince was discovered at Khoh, near Parasmania in the Nagod State of the Baghelkhand Political Agency and was issued in G.E. 156= 475-76 A.D. Hastin even assumed the royal prerogative of issuing coins in his own name and five silver coins bearing his name are preserved in the Indian Museum, Calcutta.[2] Hastin and his son Saṁkṣobha continued to issue grants of

---

[1] *Journal of the Bombay Branch of the Royal* [illegible] *Society, Vol. XX, pp. 4-5.*

[2] V. A. Smith—*Catalogue of coins in the Ind*[illegible]*seum, Vol. I, pp. 118.*

land in their own names up to G.E. 209=518-19 A.D., when the Guptas had long ceased to have any real power in Central India. Up to their last known date the Parivrājakas continued to render nominal homage to the Gupta dynasty by mentioning the name Gupta at the beginning: "In the enjoyment of sovereignty by the Gupta kings, in the glorious, augmenting and victorious reign." [1] This prerogative was usurped for the first time in the history of the Gupta empire by a feudatory chief named Lakṣmaṇa in G.E. 158=477-78 A.D. Though Lakṣmaṇa used the Gupta era he does not mention the Gupta Imperial family or any particular emperor by name.[2] The process of dissolution of the Gupta empire may therefore be stated definitely to have started immediately after the death of the emperor Skandagupta. It lasted till the death of the emperor Budhagupta or at the latest till the battle Eran in G.E. 191=510-11 A.D. Early in the 6th century the vast empire of Candragupta II and Kumāragupta I became divided into a number of petty kingdoms, among which the most important were :—

1. The later Guptas of Magadha.
2. The Maukharis of Kānyakubja.
3. The Vardhanas of Thanesar.
4. The Guptas of Eastern Mālava,

---

[1] *Gupta Inscriptions, pp. 114-15.*

[2] *Epi. Ind., Vol. II., pp. 363-65.*

5. The Hūṇas of the Punjab and Rajputana, and
6. The Maitrakas of Valabhi.

There were minor powers in all parts of the country; such as, the dynasty of Puṣpabhūti in Assam, the petty chiefs of Karṇasuvarṇa in Western Bengal, etc. None of these dynasties attained the magnitude and magnificence of the Imperial Guptas. The more ambitious among their princes founded short lived empires which never lasted for more than one generation. Such were the empires of Harṣavardhana of Thanesar and Yāśodharman of Mālava. For three centuries Northern India was plunged into a chaos from which it emerged once more as an united empire under the Hinduised Gujars of Rajputana in the first half of the 9th century A.D.

APPENDIX I.

THE TUMAIN AND MANDASOR INSCRIPTIONS.

The writer is indebted to Mr. M. B. Garde for the following information about the Tumain inscription of G.E. 116 and the newly discovered Mandasor inscription of V.S. 524. Mr. Garde will edit both of these inscriptions at some subsequent date :—

Tumain Inscription of G.E. 116.—This record does not mention Govindagupta at all. It mentions Candragupta II, Kumāragupta I, and then a prince of chief named Ghaṭotkacagupta. This Ghaṭotkacagupta cannot be the father of Candragupta I as he was living in G.E. 116. Unfortunately that portion of the inscription which recorded the relationship of Ghaṭotkacagupta to Kumāragupta I is not preserved and therefore it is extremely difficult to say in what relation they stood. It is possible that this Ghaṭotkacagupta was either a younger brother or son of Kumāragupta I and was the governor of Mālava at that time.

The Mandasor inscription of V.S. 524.—It is not quite clear from the wording of this inscription whether Govindagupta was alive in V.S. 524=467 A.D. or not. The inscription records the erection of a *Stūpa* and an *Ārāma* and the excavation of a well (*Kūpa*) by one Dattabhaṭa, son of Vāyurakṣita, who was the general of Govindagupta. Further, this Dattabhaṭa is styled the Commander-in-chief of a king named Prabhākara who is called "The destroyer of the enemies of the Gupta dynasty" (*Gupt-ānvay-āri-druma-dhumaketuḥ*). King Prabhākara is not known to us from any other source. He appears to have been a local chief or the Governor of Daśapura or Mandasor. This inscription passes over Kumāragupta I and Skandagupta, which may indicate that Govindagupta or the chiefs of Mālava did not recognise these two emperors.

APPENDIX II.

Mathura Pillar Inscription of the time of Candragupta II of the year 61.

The writer is indebted to Mr. D. B. Diskalkar, M.A., Curator, of the Mathura Museum for the following information regarding an inscription of Candragupta II discovered in a garden near the Hardinge Gate of Mathura city by Rai Bahadur Pandit Radha Krishna, the practical founder of the Mathura Museum and his nephew Pandit Bhola Nath. The record is inscribed on a small stone plllar square in section at the bottom but octagonal in the middle. The inscription covers five out of eight faces of the octagonal shaft and consists of seventeen lines. It is damaged in different parts, the most regrettable damage being to the part which bore the date in regnal years, as this is the only inscription of the early Gupta emperors, which was dated both in the Gupta era and in a regnal year. The inscription is Śaiva and on one side of the pillar is to be found a naked figure of a *Śivagaṇa* (which Mr. Diskalkar takes to be that of *Bhairava*).

The inscription opens with the name of the Bhaṭṭāraka-Mahārāja-Rājādhirāja Candragupta, the worthy son (*sat-putra*) of the Bhaṭṭarāka-Mahārāja-Rājādhirāja Samudra-gupta. The date in the Gupta era is expressed both in numerals as well as in words. The object of this inscription is to record the building of Śaiva temple, named Kapileśvara by a Śaiva ascetic in which the latter dedicated a statue (?) of his spiritual preceptor. The last portion of the inscription contains a request to the emperor to protect the grant made for the worship of the deity and for charity at the temple.

The great importance of the record lies in the fact that it supplies us with a very early date in the reign of

Candragupta II as G.E. 61=380-81 was hitherto supposed to fall in the reign of Saṁudragupta. The discovery of Rāmagupta in the *Devī-Candraguptīyam* of Viśākhadatta proves that there was some interval, however little, between Samudragupta and Candragupta II. It appears now that the late Dr. V. A. Smith was substantially correct in assigning c. 375 A.D. as the date of the accession of Candragupta II, though at that time the oldest known date of Candragupta II was G.E. 82=401-2 A.D. Samudragupta's death and Rāmagupta's accession may therefore be placed tentatively in c. 370 A.D.

CHAPTER II.

THE SYSTEM OF ADMINISTRATION AND PEERAGE.

Immediately after the fall of the Kuṣāṇa empire the system of administration and the bureaucracy underwent a great change. In the Benares inscription of the third year of Kāṇiṣka I we are introduced to a Viceroy and a Governor who were most probably in charge of the North-eastern provinces of the Scythian empire. The Viceroy was styled *Mahākṣatrapa* and the Governor *Kṣatrapa*. This inscription, therefore, proves that the Scythians had changed the names of the great officers after their conquest of India. The Maurya bureaucracy, a glimpse of which is to be obtained in the *Artha-śāstra* of Kauṭilya, was therefore changed, at least to some extent. It was not changed entirely because nearly fourteen centuries after the fall of the Maurya empire *Mahāmātras* continued to be appointed in Magadha. In the 12th century A.D., a *Mahāmātra* named Ḍallahāpiccha dedicated an image of a Bodhisatva in Bihar town.[1] Therefore, it is evident, that either the Maurya official designations had survived to a certain extent till the Musalman conquest of the country or that it

[1] T. Bloch: *Supplementary catalogue of the Archæological collections in the Indian Museum, Calcutta*, 1910, *p. 35, No. 3794.*

had been revived by some later kings. It may have remained in force in popular vocabulary because in the Maratha country a police officer is still called a *Faujdār*. In the inscription of the Gupta emperors there is no trace of the retention of the old Maurya official terms. In the earliest inscriptions of the Gupta dynasty, the Gaya plate of the reign of Samudragupta, of G.E., 9 we come across a new series of officials. The charter was written according to the orders of an *Akṣapaṭal-ādhikṛta*. In subsequent inscriptions we become quite familiar with a class of officials called *Akṣa-paṭalikas* or *Mahākṣapaṭalikas*, but this is the first time that we hear of this class of officials in Epigraphy. The Gayā grant is a very short record but it has supplied us with a new term which has not attracted the attention of scholars up to this time. This is the word *Valat-kausham*. The translator of the record recognised it as a technical official term but was not able to offer any explanation. The existence of a new class of village officials, who had to be addressed on the occasion of a transfer of land, is very interesting. In the Allahabad pillar inscription of Samudragupta one does not expect details about the system of government of the new kingdom because it is a *praśasti*, written in the *kāvya* style in praise of the king. But in 1·24 divisions of territory, unknown to us from previous inscriptions, are mentioned. Here for the first time in Indian history we hear of the term *bhukti*, which corresponds to a modern Commissioner's division in British India, consisting of several districts, and the *viṣaya* which corresponds to the Mughal *Cāklā* or the British district. The officials mentioned in the Allahabad pillar inscription are also new to us. The composer of the inscription, Hariṣeṇa, was a *Kumārāmātya*, a *Sāndhi-vigrahika* and a *Mahādaṇḍanāyaka* and a son of the *Māhadaṇḍanāyaka* Dhruvabhūti. The superintendence of the incision of the record was entrusted to another *Māhadaṇḍanāyaka* named Tilabhaṭṭaka. The Allahabad pillar inscription therefore contains the titles of three new classes of officials :—

(1) *Kumārāmātya*, (2) *Mahādaṇḍanāyaka*[1] and (3) *Sāndhivigrahika*.

The term *Kumārāmātya* has been literally translated as "Princes' Minister."[2] But a little comparative study shows that this translation is untenable; because whatever its original meaning might have been, in the beginning of the 4th century A.D. it had acquired a new significance. In the first place we find that even the highest ministers were *Kumārāmātyas*. The Brāhmaṇa Śikhara-svāmin, who was the minister (*Mantrin*) of Candragupta II and his son Pṛthivīṣeṇa, who was the minister of Kumāragupta I, were both *Kumārā-*

[1] This title was known in the Kuṣaṇa empire; cf. Lala *Daṇḍa-nāyaka* of the Mankiala inscription of the year 18 of Kāṇiṣka I—*Journal of the Royal Asiatic Society, 1909, pp. 666.*

[2] *Annual Report of the Arch. Survey of India*, 1903-04, *Part II, p. 197 No. 3.*

mātyas.[1] During the reign of Kumāragupta I, the governor of the district of Koṭivarṣa was a *Kumārāmātya* named Vetravarman.[2] At some time during the rule of the Gupta emperors in Eastern Bengal a *Kumārāmātya* had been appointed Governor of the Suvvuṅga viṣaya, but his descendants continued to use the seal of the office of the *Kumārāmātya* even after attaining independence and a later descendant used this seal even in the 8th century.[3] The seals discovered by the late Dr. T. Bloch throw a very brilliant flood of light on the bureaucracy of the Gupta empire, and especially on the different classifications in the ranks of *Kumārāmātyas*. Bloch discovered only three specimens of seals of ordinary *Kumārāmātyas*. On these seals the figure of Lakṣmī, standing inside a lotus-pond, attended by two dwarfs holding objects, which look like moneybags, occupies the upper halves. The legend on these seals is simply *Kumārāmāty-ādhikaraṇasya*. Dr. Vogel's brilliant suggestion now enables us to translate it as "(The seal) of the office of the *Kumārāmātya*."[4] At the same place 28 seals were discovered of the next higher class of *Kumārāmātyas*. They were equal in rank to the Yuvarāja, or a prince of the royal family. The term *pādīya* was not translated by Dr. Vogel; it means "equal to." *Pada* is used

---

1 *Epi. Ind. Vol. X pp. 71-72.* 2 *Ibid., Vol. XV pp. 130-133.*

3 *Ibid., pp. 306-12.*

4 *Annual report of the Archæological Survey of India,* 1903-4, *p. 107, Note* 1.

often in the same sense as *kalpa*. *Guru-pāda* is the same as *guru-kalpa* and means "one equal in rank to a preceptor." There is some difficulty in translating the word *Yuvarāja*, because in the next class of *Kumārāmātyas* we find the use of the term *Yuvarāja-bhaṭṭāraka*. Evidently there were two different classes of *Yuvarājas*. Ordinarily *Yuvarāja* means a heir-apparent, but the use of *Bhaṭṭāraka* along with *Yuvarāja* distinctly indicates two different classes. As there can be only one heir-apparent in a kingdom or empire, such a distinction can only mean that the younger princes of the royal family had also come to be styled *Yuvarājas*, while the real heir-apparent was styled *Yuvarāja-bhaṭṭāraka*. It is evident, therefore, that some of the *Kumārāmātyas* were held to be equal in rank to princes of the blood royal like the *princes* of the Roman Empire or even the Holy Roman Empire. The legends on these seals is *Yuvarāja-pādīya-Kumārāmāty-ādhikaraṇasya*, "(the seal) of the office of the *Kumārāmātya* equal in rank to a prince." The legend of the third class of *Kumārāmātyas* indicates that officers of this rank were held to be equal to the heir to the empire. Twelve specimens of seals of official of this class were discovered. In the seals of the second class we find the figure of Lakṣmī with an elephant on each side, but without any attendant.[1] In third class we see Lakṣmī with the elephants and two dwarfs

[1] *Ibid.*, No. 2.

holding round pots from which they are pouring out small objects, evidently coins.[1] The legends on the seals of the third class is *Śrī-Yuvarāja-bhaṭṭāraka-pādīya-Kumārāmāty-ādhikaraṇasya.* "(The seal) of the office of the *Kumārāmātya*, equal in rank to the illustrious heir-apparent." In the fourth or the last class of *Kumārāmātyas* the legends make a startling revelation. Only one specimen of this particular kind was discovered by Bloch at Vaiśālī. The legend runs: *Śrī-paramabhaṭṭāraka-pādīya-Kumaramātyadhikaraṇasya*; "(The seal) of the office of the *Kumārāmātya*, equal in rank to His Majesty (the Emperor)."[2] Up to this time officials of the state equal in rank to the sovereign have not been met with in ancient or modern histories. There are other officials equal in rank to the heir-apparent but none except the *Kumārāmātyas* were sufficiently high in rank to be equal to His Majesty the Emperor. The Commander-in-chief was held to be equal in rank to the heir-apparent. Only one specimen of a seal of this particular type was discovered at Vaiśālī. On this we see a vase or *kalasa* in the centre, a conch to the right and the letter *Śrī* to the left. The legend thereon is *Śrī-Yuvarāja-bhaṭṭāraka-pādīya-bal-ādhikaraṇasya*: "(the seal) of the office of the Commander-in-chief, equal in rank to the heir-apparent.[3]"

Among the higher class of officials the *Uparikas*

[1] *Ibid.*, No. 6. [2] *Ibid.*, p. 108, No. 8. [3] *Ibid.*, No. 12.

were appointed Viceroys of the provinces. Bloch discovered two seals of the *Uparika* of Tīrabhukti or Tirhut. The legend is *Tīrabhukty=Uparik-ādhikaraṇasya*. "(The seal) of the office of the *Uparika* of Tīrabhukti." The importance of the ranks of the *Uparikas* was not understood till the discovery of the Damodarpur plates. From these inscriptions we learn that the *Uparikas* were viceroys of provinces. In G.E. 124, during the reign of Kumāragupta I an *Uparika* named Cirātadatta was governing the *Bhukti* of Puṇḍravarddhana.[1] He was also in charge of the same province, *i.e.*, Northern Bengal, in G.E. 129.[2] In G.E. 163, during the reign of the Emperor Budhagupta, an *Uparika* with the title of *Mahārāja* was the Viceroy of Northern Bengal.[3] At some other time during the reign of the same Emperor another *Uparika* with the title of *Mahārāja* named Jayadatta was the Viceroy of the same province.[4] We can say now that the seals discovered by Bloch at Vaiśali were those of the Viceroys of Tīrabhukti or North Bihar.

Among the minor officials of the Gupta Empire, the Vaiśālī seals have made us familiar with many. The most noteworthy among them was an official in charge of the morals of the province of Tīrabhukti. Only one specimen of the seal of this official was discovered by Bloch. The legend is *Tīrabhuktau Vinaya-sthiti-sthāpak-ādhikaraṇa-*

[1] *Epi. Ind. Vol. XV, p. 130.*
[2] *Ibid., p. 133.*
[3] *Ibid., p. 136.*
[4] *Ibid., p. 138.*

sya. "(The seal) of the office of the Controller of morals in Tīrabhukti." Bloch suggested rightly that this Controller of Morals was an official corresponding to the Censor of Public Morals (*Dharma-Mahāmātras*) of Aśoka. The existence of such an official in the fourth and fifth centuries A.D. is extremely interesting, but the construction of the legend is rather difficult. It cannot be understood for what reasons two almost similar terms, *sthiti* and *sthāpaka*, were used in the case of the designation of one and the same officer. It may only mean that the controller of Morals was "the founder of the permanence of Morals in Tīrabhukti."[1] Among minor offices may be mentioned that of the officer-in-charge of Military Stores, corresponding to the modern Master-General of Stores; *Śrī-raṇa-bhāṇḍāgār-ādhikaraṇasya.*[2] The office of the Chief of Police had also a separate seal; *Daṇḍa-pāś-ādhikaraṇasya.*[3] It appears that the name Tīra-bhukti was originally used separated. *Bhukti* denotes a Division and the original name of Northern Bihar was Tīra and not the compound Tīra-bhukti, as in modern times, from which Tirhut has been derived. On the seal of the *Kumārāmātya* in charge of the *viṣaya of* Tīra the original name is used: *Tīra-Kumārāmaty-ādhikaraṇasya.*[4] Seals appear to have been used in

---

[1] *Annual Report of the Archæological Survey of India, 1903-4, p. 109, No. 21.*

[2] *Ibid., p. 108, No. 13.* [3] *Ibid., No. 14.*

[4] *Ibid., p. 109, No. 22.*

documents in the place of signatures. This can be proved by the large number of inscriptions on the same lump of clay in the case of agreements. In one or two cases names of officials occur along with their designations on seals. Vinayaśūra was the Chief Prefect of Police and held the rank of a *Taravara* in addition; *Mahāpartīhāra-Taravara-Vinayaśūrasya.*[1] Agnigupta was the principal judge; (*Mahādaṇḍanāyaka*).[2] Yakṣavatsa was the Commandant of the irregular cavalry; *Bhaṭ=aśvapati Yakṣavatsasya.*[3]

The system of administration has been made clear to us to some extent by the discovery of the Damodarpur plates. Under the Viceroy Cirātadatta of Puṇḍravardhana there was a *Kumārāmātya* in each district or *Viṣaya*. Vetravarman was the officer-in-charge of the district of Koṭivarṣa in G.E. 124 and 129. But in 163, under the Viceroy Brahmadatta, no minor official is mentioned as officer-in-charge of the same district. In the same reign under the Viceroy Jayadatta an officer with the rank of *Āyuktaka* named Śagaṇḍaka was the officer-in-charge of this district.[4] The *Āyuktakas* are familiar to us as *Tad-āyuktakas* and *Viniyuktakas* in mediaeval copper plates. One seal of a class of similar officials styled Prāyuktakas was discovered at Vaiśali. Ordinarily the officer-in-charge of a district was styled *Viṣaya-pati*. In the year G.E. 224,

---

[1] *Ibid., No. 16,* [2] *Ibid., p. 109, No. 17*; but see *ante. p. 69.*
[3] *Ibid., No. 18.* [4] *Ibid.. p. 138.*

during the reign of the Emperor Bhānugupta, when Rājaputradeva was the viceroy of Northern Bengal, a *Viṣaya-pati* named Svayambhu-deva was the officer-in-charge of the district of Koṭivarṣa. [1] In G.E. 146 a Viṣayapati named Śarvanāga was the officer-in-charge of the *Antarvedī* or the country between the Ganges and the Jumna.[2] In G.E. 165 a viceroy, with the title of *Mahārāja*, named Suraśmi-candra was governing that part of Central India which lies between the Jumna and the Narmadā. The actual term used is Kalindi for the Jumna and this may mean the Kali-Sindh.[3] Under Suraśmi-candra there was another official with the same title named Mātṛ-viṣṇu, who was probably the governor of Eastern Mālava or the district of Airakiṇa or Eran in the Sagar district. Finally there was Parṇadatta, Skandagupta's viceroy of Kathiawad, in whose time the dam of the great Sudarśana Lake was again rebuilt, but the Junagadh inscription does not provide us with the rank and titles of this officer. In the Gupta inscriptions we find that each province was divided into a number of revenue divisions called *Viṣayas*. The later sub-division of a province into *Maṇḍalas* and each *maṇḍala* into different *viṣayas* is yet not known. Therefore the term *viṣaya* has been translated as a district and not as a *parganah*.

The Damodarpur plates throw strong light on the administration of the districts. Five different

1 *Ibid.*, p. 142. 2 *Gupta Inscriptions*, p. 70.
3 *Ibid.*, p. 89.

classes of officials are mentioned if four of them as being associated in the government of a district. In the plate dated G.E. 124 we find mention of the *Nagara-śreṣṭhin* Dhṛtipāla, the *Sārtthavāha* Bandhumitra, the *Prathama-kulika* Dhṛtimitra, *Prathama-kāyastha* Sāmbapāla and three *Pustapālas* named Ṛṣidatta, Jayanandin and Vibhudatta. Among these the *Nagara-śreṣṭhin* still survives in Gujarat. The *Prathama-Kulika* was evidently the president of the corporation of bankers. On the analogy of the Faridpur plates of the time of Dharmāditya and Goparāja it may be stated that the *Prathama-kāyastha* was the same as the *Jyeṣṭha-kāyastha*. It is impossible to ascertain whether this post was elective or not. Most probably this officer was the head clerk of the district office. The *Sārthavāha* was a caravān-leader and we have met with the name in Kuṣāṇa inscriptions. From the existence of a large number of seals bearing the legend *Sreṣṭhi-Sārthavāha-Kulika-Nigama* discovered at Vaiśālī we may imagine that the *Sārthavāhas* mentioned in the Damodarpur plates was the Chief of the Caravan-leaders. The *Pustapālas* are new to us and were met with for the first time in the Faridpur plates. Their principal duties appear to have been the valuation of land. In the Faridpur plates only one *Pustapāla* is mentioned in each case but in the case of the Damodarpur plates we find three of them acting as a board. In the plate dated G. E. 129 the same officers, elective or appointed, are mentioned. Things are different in the plate of G.E. 163 of the reign of Budhagupta. In this case officers are not mentioned in detail but simply as the eight chief officials, such as the *Mahattara*, etc. One *Pustapāla*, only named Patradāsa, is mentioned. The officials mentioned in the second Damodarpur plate of the reign of the Emperor Budhagupta mentions Ṛbhupāla as the *Nagara-śreṣṭhin*, Vasumitra as the Caravan-leader, Varadatta as the Principal Banker or *Prathama-kulika* and Viprapāla as the Head clerk or *Prathama-Kāyastha.* In this case also we find a board consisting of three *Pustapālas*, Viṣṇudatta, Vijayanandin and Sthāṇunandin measuring out the land. In the next generation, in G.E. 224, during the reign of the Emperor Bhānugupta we find Ṛbhupāla still alive and still holding the post of the *Nagara-śreṣṭhin.* The officials mentioned are the same. The *Nagara-śreṣthin* Ṛbhupāla, the *Sārthavāha* Sthāṇudatta, the *Prathama-kulika* Matidatta and the *Prathma-Kāyastha* Skandapāla. In this case also there was a board consisting of Naranandin, Gopadatta and Bhaṭanandin but they are called *Prathama-Pustapālas.*

The Damodarpur plates throw interesting light on the conditions prevailing in Northern Bengal from the middle of the 5th to that of the 6th century A.D. The inscriptions on them are not merely grants of land and therefore they are slightly different from the later copper plate grants. They are really deeds of transfer of property. In the case of the earliest of them we find that in G.E. 124 =

443-4 A.D. a Brāhmaṇa named Karpaṭika applied for a gift of some untilled land at the same time promising to pay the price at the rate of three Dīnāras or gold coins as the price of each *Kulyavāpa*. One *Kulyavāpa* of land was given by the charter engraved on this plate according to this application. The translator of this inscription states that the land was given to him after the payment of the money. So also, in G.E. 129= 448-9 A.D. some one, whose name cannot be read at present, applied for a similar grant of land and five *Droṇa* measures were sold to him on receipt of the money. The first applicant Karpaṭika wanted the land for the performance of *Agnihotras* and the unknown applicant of the second plate wanted the land for the performance of the five great sacrifices (*Mahāyajñas*). In the case of the third plate a village head man (*Grāmika*) named Nābhaka applied for the sale of some land to settle some distinguished Brāhmaṇas. Upon the recommendation of the *Pustapāla*, Patradāsa, on the receipt of the money from the hands of Nābhaka and after inspection by village officials, one *Kulyavāpa* of uncultivated (*Khila*) land, measuring eight by nine *Nalas*, was sold to him. In this case three other men named Sthāyapāla, Kapila and Śribhadra are mentioned but the decay of the inscription did not permit the learned decipherer to connect them with the rest of the narrative. In the fourth plate from Damodarpur, which also belongs to the reign of Budhagupta, an application is made by the *Nagara-śreṣṭhin* Ṛbhupāla for the sale of some habitable land for building two temples and two store rooms. In his application Ṛbhupāla states that "in the village of Ḍoṅgā, in Himavac-chikhara (the summit of the Himalayas) I have formerly given four *Kulyavāpas* of land to the god Kokāmukha-svāmin and seven *Kulyavāpas* to the god Śveta-Varāha-svāmin. Now in the neighbourhood of these cultivated pieces of land I wish to build two temples with store-houses for these two gods." The application was granted and some building-land sold to the *Nagara-śreṣṭhin* when it had been reported by a board of three *Pustapālas* that eleven *Kulyavāpas* of land had been actually given by the former to these two gods. We learn from the fifth plate that a nobleman (*Kula-putra*) of Ayodhyā named Amṛtadeva applied for the sale of some uncultivated land for being converted into a religious trust for the repairs to and the supply of necessaries of the worship of the god Śveta-Varāha svāmin in the temple in the forest in this locality. According to this application five *Kulyavāpas* of land were sold to the applicant after taking fifteen Dināras from him. These five *Kulyavāpas* consisted of uncultivated fields along with building-lands (*vāstu*). In this case the inscription records that the land was given to the god Śveta-Varāha-svāmin. Therefore, the fifth Damodarpur plate is not merely a deed of transfer land by the State to a private individual but a grant of land to a god as well.

In the third, and fifth plates from Damodarpur it is stated in the report of the *Pustapālas* that "the land may be given for the increase of the merit of His Majesty the King (*Paramabhaṭṭāraka-Mahārāja-pādena puṇyopacayāya*). Unfortunately the seal has been preserved in the case of the fifth plate only and on this we find the legend *Kotivarṣ-ādhiṣṭhān-ādhikaraṇasya*; "(the seal) of the office of the administration of Kotivarṣa." We may compare with this the seal on the Faridpur plates, *Vāraka-maṇḍal-ādhikaraṇasya*;" (the seal) of the office of the *maṇḍala* of Vāraka." The seal as well as the form of the inscription prove that neither the Damodarpur plates nor the Faridpnr plates are Royal or Imperial grants of land. They are simply deeds of transfer of land issued by local officials in distant parts of the Empire and were transactions in which the Imperial Secretariat took no part. It cannot be understood how their Majesties Budhagupta and Bhānugupta acquired merit by selling uncultivated lands after taking the proper price.

The deeds of transfers of land on the Damodarpur plates brings us to another interesting subject, ordinary civil contracts. The seals discovered by Bloch at Vaisali contain 274 specimens bearing the legend, *Śreṣṭhi-Sārtthavāha-Kulika-Nigama*, which was correctly translated by the discoverer as "the corporation of bankers, traders (*and*) merchants." These seals are found in combination with two, three or even four others. In these cases the same lump of clay bears two three or even four impressions. The word *Nigama* means a corporation or guild and the name is to be found as early as the first century B.C. on Guild-tokens described by Cunningham.[1] But in the Nasik cave inscription of the year 42 and 45 the terms used for guilds are *Śreṇī* and *Nikāya.* It should be noticed that the same inscription also contains the word *Nigama-sabhā* which was been translated by Senart as "the town's hall."[2] In the case of a Bharhut inscription Lüders translates the same term as a town.[3] But it is extremely difficult even to conceive a town of merchants, traders and bankers only. *Nigama-sabhā* seems to have corresponded to the Guild-Halls of Modern Europe. The interest attached to the seals of this corporation of merchants, traders and bankers lies principally in their occurrence jointly with seals of other officials and private persons. In the majority of cases one separate seal contains an invocation to some deity; "Victorious be the lord Ananta with the goddess Ambā," "victory to god" "adoration to Paśupati" or "adoration to him." On the same lump, on which the seal of the Corporation and the seal bearing the invocation are to be found, we find other seals bearing the names of officials and one or more private persons. One such lump bears on it the seal of the office of a *Kumārāmātya* equal in

---

1 Cunningham: *Coins of Ancient India, p. 63, pl. III 8-9.*

2 *Epi. Ind. Vol. VIII, pp. 82-3.*

3 *Ibid., Vol. X, App. p. 67 No. 705.*

rank to the younger princes. In many cases the names of more than one person are to be found on one and the same lump of clay. The seals of Mātṛdāsa and Satyāśrita are to be found on the same seal on which are to be seen the invocation, *namastasmai*, and the seal of the Corporation of merchants, traders and bankers. That such guilds were not confined to Vaiśālī or Tīrabhukti is proved by the discovery of a seal with an almost similar legend at Bhita in the Allahabad district. In the case of the Bhita seal the legend was wrongly translated by Dr. Vogel, who regarded the term *Kulika* as "a special tribe employed as captains of mercenaries."[1] On this Spooner very pertinently observed, "the expressions 'Bankers, traders and merchants' is a homogeneous and consistent compound; 'Bankers, traders and captains' of mercenaries would seem to involve an incongruity."[2] From a distance of fifteen centuries it is very difficult to understand what this combined corporation of bankers, traders and merchants was. After the destruction of all guilds and corporations in Northern India during six centuries of Musalman rule it is not possible even to guess what they were like. It is not possible even to apply the analogy of such institutions in Gujarat where some such have survived. In old cities like Ahmadabad there are guilds and its

---

[1] *Annual Report of the Archæological Survey of India, 1911-12, p. 56, No. 55.*

[2] *Ibid., 1913-14, p. 108.*

office-bearers. The *Nagara-śreṣṭhin* of Ahmadabad is still called *Nagar-seth* but the rank is now hereditary according to Prof. A. B. Dhruva, Pro-Vice-chancellor of the Benares Hindu University, who is an inhabitant of that city. According to the same authority Gujarat guilds are now styled *Mahajans.* The *Nagara-śreśṭhin* of a city like Vaiśālī was probably the president and the chief executive officer of the great corporation. Under this great corporation there were three separate guilds for Bankers, traders and merchants. The seals discovered at Vaiśālī by Spooner prove that there was at least one separate guild of *Sreṣṭhins* or Merchants in that city, while Marshall's Bhita finds prove the existence of a separate guild of Kulikas. The term *Kulika* is perhaps better suited for translation as bankers than the term *Śreṣṭhin.* Spooner discovered several seals of the *Śreṣṭhi-nigama,*[1] at Vaiśālī and he observes that "it is noticeable that this seal is never impressed alone; some personal seal impression always accompanies it." The seals discovered by Bloch and Spooner at Vaiśālī contain the seals of a number of Chief *Kulikas* such as *Prathama-Kulik-Ograsiṅha* and *Prathama-Kulika-Hariḥ.*[2] The existence of *Prathama-Kulikas* at Koṭivarṣa in Northern Bengal and at Vaiśālī proves that this office was also a regular institution in North-eastern India if not in the whole of Northern India. The distinction between a *Prathama-*

[1] *Ibid., pp. 125, No. 8 B; 137 No. 270A; 150, No. 648; 158, No. 804.*

[2] *Ibid., p. 139, No. 277 A; 1903-4, p. 117, Nos. 99–160.*

Kulika and ordinary Kulikas is evident and many of seals of ordinary *Kulikas* were discovered at Vaiśālī. With regards to the *Sārthavāhas* we do not possess any evidence of the existence of any guild or organisation. Spooner discovered an unique seal of another *Nigama* but he could not read the legend definitely. According to him it reads *Makkupali-Nigamasya.*[1]

Sir Aurel Stein has proved from his discoveries in Central Asia that the Ancient Indian envelope consisted of two boards tied together with a string or wire, to the knot of which a lump of clay was attached. The seal of the person sending a letter was attached or impressed to this lump of clay. The fact that the majority of seals discovered were fired proves that in the majority of cases the binding material of Ancient Indian envelopes was something that would not burn when the clay seal was fired.

Lumps of clay bearing two or even three impressions of seals of private persons may mean a joint petition to some officer of Vaiśālī, but when we find that the seal of the great Corporation of Bankers, traders and merchants affixed to the same lump of clay with the seal of the office of a *Kumārāmātya* equal in rank to a prince of the blood-royal what are we to conclude except that it was the seal attached to a contract between these people and the great *Kumārāmātya* ?[2] The small chamber

---

[1] *Ibid., 1913-14, p. 127 No. 64A.* [2] *Ibid., 1903-4, p. 110, No. 29.*

in which Bloch discovered the seals is generally considered to be either the record room of the royal offices at Vāiśālī or the lumber room of some office. Therefore it may be taken that seals with the impression of the great corporation along with those of one or more private persons are really seals attached to petitions addressed to some officials, but in my opinion such an explanation is untenable because there can hardly be any necessity for a great guild to apply jointly with private persons, specially in cases where such persons were members of the great Corporation or a subordinate guild. It appears to me that lumps bearing the impression of the seal of the great Corporation of Bankers, merchants and traders, an invocation and one or more private seals are really seals attached to contracts between one or more parties. Let us take for example 15 specimens of the seal of Prakāśanandin, out of which two were found combined with that of the office of the provincial government of Vaiśālī: *Vaiśāly=adhiṣṭhān=ādhikaraṇaḥ*. There cannot be any other explanation of this seal save and except that it was a contract between Prakāśnandin and the government which was brought and deposited in the government record office or was thrown away when the contract was no longer subsisting.[1] It cannot be imagined that the office of the government of Vaiśālī sent a petition jointly with a private person named Prakāśa-

---

[1] *Ibid., p. 117, No. 96.*

nandin to some higher officials. Let us take another example. Out of 27 seals of a private person named Nāgasiṁha, one is combined with the seal of the Corporation of Bankers, traders and merchants and another private person named Bhavasena. In this case also it appears that the seal was attached to a private contract to which the great Corporation was a party and which was brought to the government record office for registration. Arrangements for registration by governments in Ancient India, in ages later than the Gupta period, are far too numerous. We have therefore to admit that out of 274 specimens of the seal of the great Corporation of Bankers, traders and merchants at least 254 were attached to contracts brought to the government office of Vaiśālī for registration and safe custody.

In the Gupta period, as well as earlier periods, according to the discoveries of Spooner at Vaiśālī, clay was the ordinary material used for sealing. Such seals were used both for covers of contracts as well as of letters. In the case of documents intended for permanent record copper or silver was used. Instances of copper seals are those attached to the Gaya plate of Samudragupta of G.E. 9 = 328-9 A.D., the seal of the government of the district of Koṭivarṣa and that of the *maṇḍala* of Vāraka from Faridpur.[1] The only instance known to us in which silver was used for sealing is that of

[1] *Ind. Ant. Vol. XXXIX, 1910, pp. 193-205, pl. II.*

the great seal of Kumāragupta II discovered at Saiyadpur-Bhitari in the Ghazipur district of the U.P. Bloch described the clay seals and the method of sealing in the following words;—"From the shape of the clay pieces it is evident that they were attached to letters or other literary documents, and that they served to hold together the string which was tied around the wooden boards upon which the letter was written, or which were used as a sort of envelope. In that case either birch-bark or palm-leaf took the place of our modern paper. Fig. 18 gives a view of the reverse of one of the clay lumps. The method adopted for sealing letters at this time seems to have been to press down the ends of the string tied round the boards into a piece of moist clay by means of some instrument, perhaps the broad side of a knife. Evidence of this is the groove which invariably occurs on the back of all the seals. Generally a few thin lines run across its centre. They must have been made by the blunt edge of the knife to press down the strings more deeply, in order to make them adhere tighter to the clay. The other side of the clay bears the impression of the sender's seal. In many cases traces remains of the finger-marks of the persons who handled the seals while moist. As the majority consisted of pieces of unbaked clay, it is clear that it was considered sufficient to allow the seal to dry during the transit of the letter. A few pieces are of a light yellow colour, and look as if the seal had been heated a little before despatching the letter. The present find thus distinguishes itself sharply from other collections of clay seals made at various ancient Indian sites, which as a rule consist of votive tablets, either put down as offerings near holy shrines or taken away as memorials by pilgrims. The reverse of the latter is invariably quite smooth, and the groove and stringholes seen on all the Basarh seals are entirely wanting."[1]

The emblems used on these seals is extremely interesting. Garuḍa, the vehicle of Viṣṇu was the emblem or *Lāñchana* of the Imperial Gupta family. This will be seen in the upper part of the silver seal of Kumāragupta II and that attached to the Gayā plate of Samudragupta. Fleet regarded the seal as genuine but thought that the inscription on the plate was forged.[2] Evidently the ladies of the Imperial house did not use the emblem of the Gupta family because on the seal of the Great Queen Dhruvasvāminī discovered by Bloch at Vaiśālī we find a seated lion facing right above the legend. On this seal Dhruvadevī or Dhruva-svāmini is called "the wife of the Mahārājādhirāja, the illustrious Candragupta, the mother of the Mahārāja, the illustrious Govindagupta." In the case of the official seals the figure of Lakṣmī predominates. In the case of the four different classes of Kumārāmātyas the standing figure of Lākṣmī with

---

1 *Annual Report of the Archæological Survey of India, 1903-4, pp. 101-2.*

2 *Gupta Inscriptions, pl. XXXVII.*

or without attendants is always present. But in the case of the Commander-in-chief, equal in rank to the Heir-apparent, the place of Lakṣmī is taken by a vase. On the seal of the office of the Master-General of Military Stores the figure of Lakṣmī attended by elephants and dwarfs once more occupy the central space. The private seals of officials do not bear the official *lāñchana*; symbols of the Sun and Moon on that of Vinayaśūra, a humped bull couchant in the case of the judge Agnigupta and a boar and a conch with the symbols of the Sun and Moon on that of Yakṣavatsa. In the case of provincial officials Lakṣmī with elephants and dwarfs appear on the seals of the more important offices; the seal of the viceroy or *Uparika* of Tīrabhukti, the Censor of Public Morals of the same province and that of the *Kumārāmātya* of the province. But the *lāñchana* is quite different in the case of the office of the government of (the city of) Vaiśālī where we find a hemispherical object, "perhaps money-chest," and that of the office of the district (*viṣaya*) of Vaiśālī in which case we get a wheel with symbols of the Sun and the Moon. Spooner discovered a seal of the office of a court of law with the legend *Dharmmāsan-ādhikaraṇasya* in which case the *lāñchana* is a tall vase.[1] Among the few official seals discovered by Spooner the most important is the unique seal of a new class of *Kumārāmātyas*. The legend is *Vaiśālī-nāma-kuṇḍe*

[1] *Annual Report of the Archæological Survey of India, 1913-14*, pp. 127-8, No. 69 A.

Kumārāmāty-ādhikaraṇasya; but it is impossible to translate it because we do not know what *nāma-kuṇḍe* exactly means.[1] In this case we find Lakṣmī with elephants. It appears therefore that while Garuḍa, the vehicle of the god Viṣṇu, was the *lāñchana* of the Gupta Imperial family, Lakṣmī, the consort of that god, was the emblem of the Imperial offices. The lower provincial officials were not allowed to use it.

Inscriptions and seals indicate that in some cases at any rate ministers were hereditary. In the case of *Amātyas* we have Spooner's seal from Vaiśālī in which we see that the *Amātya* Hastabala was the son of the *Amātya* Bhadrika.[2] In the reign of Candragupta II Vīrasena *alias* Śaba of Pāṭaliputra calls himself the hereditary minister as well as the minister of peace and war (*Anvaya-prāpta-Sācīvyo-vyāpṛita-Sāndhivigrahaḥ*) in the Udaygiri cave inscription.[3] The most important case of hereditary succession to offices is recorded in the Karamdanda inscription of G.E. 117=446-7 A.D. We learn from this record that the *Kumārāmātya* Śikhara-svāmin, a brāhmaṇa of the Aśva-vājī *gotra*, was the minister (*Mantrin*) of Candragupta II. But his son, the *Kumārāmātya* Pṛthivīṣeṇa was at first the *Mantrin* of the Emperor Kumāragupta I but later on he became the Commander-in-chief (*Mahābalādhikṛta*).[4]

---

1 *Ibid.*, p. 136, No. 200.

2 *Ibid.*, No. 210.

3 *Gupta Inscriptions*, p. 35.

4 *Epi. Ind.*, Vol. X, pp. 71-2.

Very little reliable data is available about the land revenue system of the early Gupta Empire. Literary evidence is altogether absent. The only sources of information are the inscriptions on copper plates of the period discovered at Dhanaidaha in the Rajshahi district and at Damodarpur in the Dinajpur district of Bengal. From the Damodarpur plates we learn that in the Puṇḍravardhana *bhukti* there was much fallow or waste land. The division of land is into (1) *Nāla* (cultivated), (2) *Khila* (fallow, waste), and (3) *Vāstu* (homestead). Applications were made for the sale of such waste lands for religious purposes. In the Damodarpur plate of G.E. 124 such waste land is called *Apradā* and *Aprahata.* These terms have been translated by the learned decipherer as "as yet unploughed and not already given." The term *Aprahata* cannot be translated as "not already given." The natural meaning is "that which is not barred in the case of transfer." So also *Apradā* means "unproductive." The Second term is used once more in the second plate of G.E. 129. Prof. Basak translates it "land of which no previous gift (*pradā*) has been made. In the light of the expression *apradā-dharmeṇa* in plate No. 5 (in the place of *Nīvī-dharmeṇa*) the phrase *apradā-kshaya* may here be explained, as in the case of *nīvi-dharma-kshaya,* thus—land could not, unless so conditioned, be alienated or transferred without state-permission, after being once sold for the purpose of a gift to a Brāhmaṇa or a god. We might equally well read the phrase as *aprad-āksh-*

aya."[1] To me it seems that *apradā-dharma* should be taken to be "the law or rules governing unproductive lands." All over the United provinces special rules and regulations govern the transfer and the income from such lands, called *Nuzul. Apradā kṣaya* should mean the disposal of unproductive lands. From the fifth Damodarpur plate we learn that there was a large amount of forest-land in the Koṭivarṣa district of the Puṇḍravardhana Division, because in his application Amṛtadeva, the nobleman of Ayodhyā, states that the temple of the god Śveta-Varāha-svāmin was situated "in this forest."[2]

Marshall's Bhita excavations yielded some very important seals. Those belonging to the Gupta period support the conclusions stated above. The official seals bear the *lāñchana* of the Gupta Empire, Lakṣmī attended by elephants and dwarfs. The best specimen is that of the office of the ordinary *Kumārāmātya.*[3] The seal of the office of the district of Sāmāharṣa is also similar, (*Sāmāharṣa-viṣay=ādhikaraṇasya*).[4] In one respect some of the seals from Bhita show a deviation from the ordinary class of Imperial official seals from Vaiśālī. In these specimens the name of a higber official is mentioned, *Mahāśvapati-Mahādaṇḍanāyaka-Viṣṇurakṣita-pādānugṛhīta-Kumārāmāty=adhikaraṇasya.* The real import of the term *pādānu-*

[1] *Ibid., Vol. XV, p. 134, Note 1.* [2] *Ibid., p. 143.*

[3] *Annual Report of the Archæological Survey of India, 1911-12, p. 53. No. 35, Pl. XIX.*

[4] *Ibid. p. 54, No. 42.*

gṛhita could not be understood in 1911-12. The Damodarpur plates have familiarised us with similar terms. Thus during the reign of Kumāragupta I the *Uparika* Cirātadatta was appointed viceroy of Puṇḍravardhana and the term used is *tat-pāda-parigṛhīte* "was accepted by His Majesty's feet" in the plates of G.E. 124 and 129. A similar term is used in the case of Budhagupta's viceroy for the same province, Brahmadatta, in the plate of G.E. 163 as well as in the case of Jayadatta in the undated plate of the time of the same Emperor. An exactly similar term is used in the plate of Rājaputradeva in the plate of G.E. 224 of the reign of Bhānugupta. Shorn of its elegance, the phrase simply means "(The seal) of the office of the *Kumārāmātya* appointed by the Cavalry-leader and general Viṣṇurakṣita."[1] In this case it is more reasonable to translate the term *Daṇḍanāyaka* as a general; *lit.* leader (*nāyaka*) of an army (*daṇḍa*). In the second instance of this class the legend is incomplete on account of breakage: it can be restored as *Mahārāja-Śaṅkarasiṁha-[pādānugṛhīta-Yuvarāja]-pādīy-Āyuktak=ādhikaraṇasya*, "(The seal), of the office of the Āyuktaka, equal in rank to a prince, appointed by Mahārāja Saṅkarasiṁha." The space in the second line indicates that this officer had some other rank in addition to that of the *Āyuktaka*, perhaps that of a *Kumārāmātya*.[2] The most important point with

[1] *Ibid.*, *p.* 52, *No.* 32, *Pl. XVIII.*

[2] *Ibid.*, p. 53, *Pl. XVIII.* This seal is upside down in the illustration.

regard to these two seals is the *lāñchana*, Lakṣmī attended by elephants. Like the Vaiśālī seals the Bhita finds contain a number of private seals of officials. The most important are the seals of a number of Ministers; *or Amātyas*; Īśvaracandra, Dharmadeva, Boḷa, Nāgadāman, Īśvarānana. So also we have the seals of a number of judges or Generals (*Daṇḍnāyaka*); Śaṅkaradatta, Grāmabala, Lāḷa, Keśavadāsa, Yajñavīrya, Uṁma, and Vaṅśa. One particular private seal is important because it contains the names of two Police officials; *Pratīhārayor-Vviśākha-Rudradāma(yoḥ)*. In this case one letter, the fifth, was omitted by the decipherer.[1] The Bhita finds have also provided us with one important class of seals, that of a Guild of the *Kulikas* or Bankers, which could not be found in the Vaiśālī collections of Bloch and Spooner. The legend is simply *Kulika-Nigamasya*.[2] It should be noted in this connection that Mr. R. G. Basak is inclined to translate the word *Kulika* as "artisan." But though the commentator Bhānuji Dīkṣita explains it as "the foremost person in a company of artisans," the explanation in the *Amarakoṣa* connects it with the *Śreṣṭhins*.[3]

Most probably the four plates from Faridpur belong to the later part of the Gupta period. They belong to the reigns of three different kings about whom nothing is known from any other source.

---

1 *Ibid.*, p. 55, No. 52, Pl. XIX.

2 *Ibid.*, p. 56, No. 55.

3 *Epi., Ind. Vol. XV. p. 131, Note 6.*

Two of them belong to the reign of a king named Dharmāditya, the third to that of Gopacandra and the fourth to that of Samācāra. Out of these three kings Samācāra is also known from a solitary gold coin identified correctly for the first time by Mr. N. K. Bhāttasali of the Dacca Museum[1] Dharmāditya may be the *Āditya* name of one of the later Gupta Kings but we cannot be too sure of this because in the Damodarpur plates all Gupta Emperors are mentioned by their proper names, which are not even followed by their *Āditya*-names. Hoernle's proposed identification of Dharmāditya with Yaśodharman need not be considered seriously like his theory of the latter being known as Vikramāditya since the publication of the Sanjan plates of Amoghavarṣa I which indicate distinctly that *Vikramāditya* belonged to the Gupta family.[2] All that can be said about these plates is that they belong to the period between 550 and 650 A.D.

In form, the inscriptions on the Faridpur plates, resemble those on the Damodarpur ones. The first plate, that of the third year of Dharmāditya records that during the reign of the *Mahārājādhiraja* Dharmāditya and during the government of the *Mahārāja* Sthāṇudatta and the period of office of the *Viṣayapati* Jajāva in the *Maṇḍala* of Vāraka, one Vātabhoga applied for the sale of some land to bestow it on a Brāhmaṇa. On the report of

---

[1] *Catalogue of the coins of the Gupta dynasties, etc. British Museum p. 150.*

[2] *Epi., Ind. Vol. XVIII, pp. 248, 255.*

the *Pustapāla* Vinayasena four *Kulyavāpas* of land were sold to Vātabhoga on receipt of 12 *Dīnaras* or gold coins. Two points in this inscription deserve special mention; (1) "There is in this district the rule established along the *Eastern sea* that cultivated lands are things which are sold according to the rate of the sum of four Dīnaras;" (2) "and then the feet of the Emperor receives the sixth part of the price according to the law here."[1] The mention of the Eastern sea bars the proposed identification of Vāraka with Varendra.[2] The gain of a sixth part of the price by His Majesty is a new feature in ancient Indian transfers of land. The land purchased by Vātabhoga was bestowed by the same inscription to a Brāhmaṇa named Candra-svāmin as in the case of the fifth Damodarpur plate, in which case the land was given to a god.

The second Faridpur plate is not dated. It records that during the reign of the Emperor Dharmāditya and the government of the Viceroy, the *Mahāpratīhāra* and *Uparika*, Nāgadeva in the New Avakāśikā, when Gopāla-svāmin was in charge of the district and *Maṇḍala* of Vāraka, a man named Vasudeva-svāmin applied for the sale of some land in order to bestow it on a Brāhmaṇa named Soma-svāmin. By this record some land was sold at the current rate of four *Dīnāras* to the *Kulyavāpa*.

The third Faridpur inscription, that of the year

---

[1] *Ind. Ant. Vol.* XXXIX, *1910, p. 197.* [2] *Ibid., p. 209.*

19 of Gopacandra, records that during the reign of this emperor and the government of the *Mahāpratīhāra*, *Kumārāmātya* and *Uparika* Nāgadeva, when Vatsapāla-svāmin was in charge of the disrict and *Maṇḍala* of Vāraka, Vatsapāla-svāmin, himself, applied for the sale of some land to bestow it on a Brāhmaṇa named Gomidatta-svāmin. In the second plate the *Pustapāla* was Janmabhūti but in the third plate the *Pustapāla* was Nayabhūti. Like the inscription on the first plate this inscription turns into a deed of gift at the end, because it states that Vatsāpala-svāmin bestowed the land purchased by him on Bhaṭṭa Gomidatta-svāmin. The second plate of the reign of Dharmāditya cannot be very far removed from the third in date because both mention the Headclerk Nayasena.[1]

The fourth plate from Faridpur belongs to the reign of the Emperor Samācāra. It records that during the government of the Viceroy, the *Antaraṅga* and *Uparika*, Jīvadatta in the New Avakāśikā, when a *Viṣayapati* named Pavittruka was in charge of the *Maṇḍala* of Vāraka, one Supratīka-svāmin applied for the sale of some land for the establishment of certain Vedic ceremonies and accordingly some land was given to this Brāhmaṇa. The inscription on the fourth plate does not record a transfer but a free gift of land.[2] The material difference in informations to be derived from the

---

1 *Ibid., pp. 204-05.*

2 *Epi. Ind. Vol. XVIII, p. 74-86.*

inscriptions on the Damodarpur and the Faridpur plates is enormous. The Damodarpur plates show a well-ordered civil government in which the Chief officer of a district was associated with the headclerk of the government offices and the three principal leaders of the mercantile community, the *Nagara-śreṣṭhin*, the *Prathama-Kulika*, and the Caravan-leader. In the majority of cases report on the land to be transferred is submitted by a board of three Pustapālas. In the four Faridpur plates the only officer who is mentioned as such is the headclerk, now styled a *Jyeṣṭha-Kāyastha* instead of *Prathama-Kāyastha*. Even this officer is omitted in the fourth plate and his place taken by a *Jyeṣṭh-ādhikaraṇika* named Dāmuka.

CHAPTER III.

Religious and Literary Revival.

The monarchs of the Gupta dynasty will be remembered for ever for the great reformation they brought about in Orthodox Hindu society and religion. From their inscriptions, coins, and seals they are distinctly Vaiṣṇavas. In the majority of their inscriptions and coins they are styled *Parama-Bhāgavata*. The emblems on their personal and official seals, Garuḍa and Lakṣmī, the vehicle and consort of Viṣṇu, also indicate that they were ardent Vaiṣṇavas. There is no indication of any of the kings from Candragupta I to Bhanugupta having leant towards any other Indian faith. They are clearly different from the Vardhanas of Thanesar in this respect. The inscriptions of the dynasty clearly indicate a revival of Hinduism or the Orthodox Brahmanical religion and a corresponding decline in the two remaining religions of India. From other inscriptions we learn that Jainism was still lingering in Mathurā but that the days of its prosperity were finally over. As no other material is available for the study of the religious history of the Gupta Empire we must return to a further study of the inscriptions of the period. There is no indication of a leaning towards any particular sect in the Allahabad pillar inscription save and except that Hariṣeṇa was a Hindu and probably a Śaiva. The fragmentary condition of the Eran pillar makes it difficult to assign it to any Hindu sect, but the sense is sufficiently clear to mark it as Hindu. The new Mathurā inscription of G.E. 61 of the reign of Candragupta II is Śaiva. The Udayagiri cave inscription of G.E. 82 is clearly non-sectarian but the carvings of the cave, which are contemporary, prove that the donor, the Sanakānīka chief, whose name is mutilated, was a Vaiṣṇava. The undated Udayagiri cave inscription of the time of Candragupta II records the dedication of a Śaiva cave-temple by his minister Vīrasena of Pāṭaliputra. The fragmentary Gaḍhwa inscription of G.E. 88 is distinctly Hindu, though the sect can not be determined. The only Buddhist inscription of the reign is the Sanchi pillar inscription of the year 93. No Jain inscriptions of the time of Samudragupta or Candragupta II have been discovered so far. The two inscriptions from Gaḍhwa, belonging to the reign Kumāragupta I, though fragmentary, are distinctly Hindu and the Bilsad pillar inscription in the Eta district of the U.P. is also Hindu. It refers to some work by a Brāhmaṇa named Dhruvaśarman in a temple of the god Mahāsena or Kārtikeya in G.E. 96. In G.E. 113=432–3 A.D. a Jain image was dedicated by a Jain lady named Sāmāḍhyā at Mathurā. This is the earliest known Jain inscription of the Gupta period. In G.E. 129 an image of Buddha was dedicated at Mankuwar in the Karchhanā *Tahsil* of the Allahabad district by a Buddhist *Bhikṣu* named Budhamitra. Three known inscriptions belonging to the reign of Kumāragupta I are on copper plates discovered in Bengal. The earliest of them, discovered at Dhanaidaha in the Rajshahi district, is very fragmentary, but is dated G.E. 113. The references to Brāhmaṇas leave no doubt about the fact that the object of the record was some contract between Hindus.[1] The first and second Damodarpur plates of G.E. 124 and 129 are distinctly Hindu or Brahmanical as they refer to *Agnihotras* and *Mahāyajñas*. The great Junagaḍh rock inscription of Skandagupta is distinctly Vaiṣṇava as it opens with an invocation to the god Viṣṇu. The second part of this inscription records the erection of a temple of Viṣṇu by Cakrapālita, son of the Viceroy Parṇadatta. The inscription on the stone pillar at Kahāuṁ in the Deoriya *Tahsil* of the Gorakhpur district is the second Jain record of the Gupta period. It records the erection by a man named Madra of a pillar with five images of the *Ādikartṛs* or *Tīrthaṅkaras* in G.E. 141. The last inscription of the time of Skandagupta is Hindu. In the copper plate discovered at Indor Khera in the Bulandshahr district, a Brāhmaṇa, named Devaviṣṇu, records the gift of some money for the maintenance of a lamp in a temple of Sūrya in G.E. 146.

In the troublesome period which followed the death of the Emperor Skandagupta and which is

---

[1] *Epi. Ind. Vol. XVII, pp. 347-8.*

occupied by the ephemeral reigns of the three shadow Emperors, we get only two inscriptions, both of which belong to the reign of the infant emperor Kumāragupta II. Only one of them is dated and that is a Buddhist inscription recording the erection of an image of Buddha in G.E. 154 during the reign of the Emperor Kumāragupta II by a Buddhist monk named Abhayamitra.[1] The great seal of Kumāragupta II discovered at Bhitari in the Ghazipur district is much bigger than the seal of Samudragupta attached to the Gayā plate of G.E. 9. It bears the complete geneology of the Gupta Emperors from Śrī-gupta to Kumāragupta II and is distinctly Vaiṣṇava on account of the presence of the figure of Garuḍa in the upper part and the term *Parama-bhāgavata* applied to Candragupta II.[2]

During the reign of Budhagupta the empire was once more re-united. The earliest inscription of Budhagupta's reign is Buddhist. It records the erection of an image of Buddha by the same Buddhist monk Abhayamitra in G.E. 157. The Damodarpur plates of the time of Budhagupta are distinctly Hindu. The third plate of G.E. 163 records the sale of some land for the settlement of some Brāhmaṇas in G.E. 163 to a village-elder named Nābhaka. The fourth plate records the sale of some *Vāstu* and *Khila* land to the *Nagara-śreṣ-*

---

1 *Annual Report of the Archæological Survey of India, 1914–15*, pp. 124–5.

2 *Journal of the Asiatic Society of Bengal, 1889, LVIII*, p. 89.

ṭhin Ṛbhupāla for building two temples for the gods Kokāmukha-svāmin and Śveta-Varāha-svāmin and the attached store-rooms. The last known inscription of the reign of Budhagupta records the erection of a flag-staff of Viṣṇu in G.E. 165 by the *Mahārāja* Mātṛviṣṇu and his brother Dhanya viṣṇu. The fifth Damodarpur plate is also a Hindu record because by it a religious trust was created in favour of the god Śveta-Varāha-svāmin in the forest of Koṭivarṣa by Amṛtadeva of Ayodhyā in G.E. 224. The Eran pillar inscription of the reign of Bhānugupta is non-sectarian. There remain a number of dated records which do not mention the names of the Emperors, but which can be referred to the reigns of well known Emperors of the Imperial Gupta dynasty. The Udayagiri cave inscription of G.E. 106 must be referred to the reign of Kumāragupta I and is a Jaina inscription. The Sanchi inscription of G.E. 131 is a record of the reign of Kumāragupta I and is a Buddhist record. It commemorates the gift of fifteen gold coins from the interest of which one Bhikṣu was to be fed daily and three lamps to be lighted in the sanctum (*Ratnagṛha*) by the lay worshipper Harisvāminī. The Mathurā image inscription, if it is to be referred to the Gupta era, of the year 135 falls within the reign of Kumāragupta I and is a Buddhist inscription. Similarly the Ḳosam image inscription of the *Mahārāja* Bhīmavarman of G.E. 139 must be referred to the reign of Skandagupta. So also the Gaḍhwa inscription of G.E. 148 must be referred to the reign of the same Emperor.

In this long list of inscriptions only four are Jaina and less than half-a-dozen Buddhist. This enormous preponderance of Hindu or Brāhmanical records prove definitely that Hinduism had benefitted greatly at the cost of the rival sects. There is one class of records which do not contain dates or names of Emperors but which can be referred to the Gupta period very definitely on the basis of palæography. These are the votive inscriptions of the Gupta period discovered during the last two decades at Sarnath, the Buddhist Benares. The Sarnath inscriptions of this period do not mention the names of Gupta Emperors except in three solitary instances, the Buddha image of the reign of Kumāragupta II of G.E. 154 and two similar images of the reign of Budhagupta of G.E. 157. Is it the beginning of the Buddhist custom of refusing to recognise a non-Buddhist King in permanent records ? The inscribed images from Sarnath, though they do not furnish any data for the political history of the Gupta period, afford us ample material for the study of the evolution of artistic activity of the Benares School of Sculpture. Incidentally they prove the truth of Fa-Hsien's statement that Buddhism continued to flourish side by side with Hinduism. The same can not be said of Jainism ; that religion was distinctly on the decline. Even in great centres of the Jaina faith like Mathurā the dedication of Jaina images in the

Gupta period was a rare event. The recent discovery of a copper plate at Paharpur in the Rajshahi district of Bengal proves that the eradication of Jainism from North-Eastern India was very rapid. According to Mr. K. N. Dikshit M.A., the discoverer, the inscription on this copper plate is dated G.E. 159=478-9 A.D. and therefore it must be referred to the reign of Budhagupta. It records the donation of some land by a Brāhmaṇa couple for the maintenance of worship in a Jaina *Vihāra* or establishment of Nirgrantha ascetics presided over by Guhanandin at the Village of Vaṭa-Gohali. This inscription does not mention the name of the reigning Emperor Budhagupta though he is expressly mentioned as such in the third Damodarpur plate of G. E. 163. A century after the fall of the Imperial Guptas, Yuan Chwang mentions naked Jaina mendicants in the temples of North Bengal. But in the Pāla period there is hardly any evidence of Jaina influence in Bengal as only half-a-dozen Jaina images have been discovered throughout the length and breadth of that province.

The preponderating influence of Hinduism over other sects in the Gupta period is felt to some extent in Sanskrit literature. The majority of the Purāṇas were recast during the Gupta period. A Purāṇa ought to consist of the following parts :—

"(1) *Sarga*, the evolution of the universe from its material cause; (2) *Pratisarga*, the recreation of the universe from the constituent elements into which it is merged at the close of each aeon (*Kalpa*) or day in the life of the Creator, Brahmā; (3) *Vamça*, the genealogies of God and Ṛishis; (4) *Manvantara*, the groups of 'great ages' (*Mahāyuga*) included in an aeon, in each of which mankind is supposed to be produced anew from a first father, Manu; (5) *Vaṁçānucharita*, the history of the Royal families who rule over the earth during the four 'ages' (*yuga*) which make up one 'great age.'"[1]

Now, only a few Purāṇas are complete with all the five divisions. Such Purāṇas which contain the *Vaṁśānucarita* prove that the majority of them were finally redacted during the Gupta period. Seven only out of the existing eighteen Mahāpurāṇas contain accounts of the kings who have reigned or who, in the prophetic form in which the authors of these works have recast their narratives, will reign in the historical period. The historical genealogies in these works are based on very ancient and reliable sources. The accounts of kings were written from the songs of heralds (*Sūtas*) of the Vedic period who, like the *Chāraṇs* of mediaeval Rajputana, were the chroniclers of the genealogies of kings and their deeds. The *Sūtas* were Kṣatriyas. But, after the fall of the Kṣatriyas, these songs, called *Gāthās* and *Nārāśaṁsīs* fell into the hands of

[1] *Cambridge History of India Vol. I. p. 296.*

Brāhmaṇa compilers, who, ignorant of the past, confused the accounts and in many cases omitted particular genealogies or left them incomplete, in order to make room for modern legends to prove the sanctity of some new holy place. Pargiter, who has analysed the Pauranic accounts very carefully, has proved that the accounts of the dynasties which followed the Andhras, are given in a very summarised form; "When the Kingdom of the Andhras has come to an end there will be kings belonging to the lineage of their servants; 7 Andhras, and 10 Ābhīra kings; also 7 Gārdabhins, 18 Śakas. There will be 8 Yavanas, 14 Tuṣāras, 13 Muruṇḍas, 11 Maunas.

"The Śrīparvātīya Andhras will endure 52 years; the 10 Ābhīra kings 67 years; the 7 Gardabhins will enjoy the earth 72 years; the 18 Śakas 183 years. The 8 Yavanas will enjoy this earth 87 years. The earth is remembered as belonging to the Tuṣāras 7000 years. The 13 future Muruṇḍas along with low caste men, all of Mleccha origin, will enjoy it 103 years. When they are overthrown by time there will be Kilakila kings.

"Then after the Kilakilas Vindhyaśakti will reign. He will enter upon the earth after it has known these kings 96 years." Different Purāṇas differ in their accounts. The *Matsya*, the *Vāyu* and the *Bhaviṣyat* give almost identical accounts and is closely followed by the *Bhāgavata*. Names are to be found again, later on, in the accounts of the Kingdom of Vidiśā. Subsequent accounts are all confused and we are presented with the following dynastic list in the fourth century A.D. :—

"Nine Nāka kings will enjoy the city Campāvatī; and 7 Nāgas will enjoy the charming city of Mathurā. Kings born of the Gupta race will enjoy all these territories, namely, along the Ganges, Prayāga, Sāketa and the Magadhas."

That the Paurānic accounts of the dynasties of the fourth century A.D., is correct can be proved from contemporary epigraphic and numismatic evidence. The last King of the Nāga dynasty of Nalapurā (Nārwar) and Padmāvatī (Pawāyā), (some of the texts of the Purāṇas read Padmāvatī, instead of Campāvāti). Gaṇapati Nāga issued copper coins, which clearly belong to the fourth century A.D. and he is mentioned in the Allahabad inscription of Samudragupta as one of the kings of Northern India, who were overthrown by that king. The account of the Gupta empire, as given in the *Vāyu*, *Bhavishyat*, *Viṣṇu* and the *Bhāgavata Purāṇas* agree with the known inscriptions. The Gupta Kingdom in its earliest stage, *e.g.*, during the reign of Samudragupta consisted of Bengal, Bihar, Eastern part of the United Provinces and perhaps a small portion of the modern Central Provinces. This kingdom consisted of the valley of the Ganges (*Anu-Gāṅga*), the valley of the Yamunā (*Prayāga*), Oudh (*Sāketa*) and

South Bihar (*Magadha*). The detailed evidence, which enabled Sir Ramakrishna Gopal Bhandarkar to reconstruct the chronology of the Andhras or the Sātavahanas, is wanting in the case of the Guptas. It is clear from the nature of the Paurānic evidence that the Guptas were the last dynasty of the kings of the middle country who were known to the final redactors of the *Matsya*, *Vāyu*, *Viṣṇu*, *Brahmāṇḍa* and the *Bhāgavata* Purāṇas. Therefore it can be stated that the final redaction of most of the reliable Purāṇas took place before the disruption of the Gupta Empire.

This final redaction of the Purāṇas was one of the minor results of the activities of the Brāhmaṇas of Northern India in the fifth and sixth centuries A.D. Their principal work was the reform of Hinduism or the Orthodox Brāhmanical religion from the state of torpor into which it had fallen during the long rule of the barbarians. The rise of Northern Buddhism during the reign of Kāṇiṣka I and the creation of a pantheon of superior and inferior deities in it had constituted that religion into a very formidable rival of Orthodox Hinduism. Deprived of Imperial patronage during the long centuries which followed the dismemberment of the Śuṅga empire, the priestly classes were unable to retard the total break-up of castes or to do anything which would make the now unintelligible religion of the Vedic Aryans more acceptable to the masses. We do not know much about the condition of the

Orthodox Brahmanical religion during the five centuries which intervened between the fall of the Imperial Śuṅgas and the rise of the Guptas. The inscriptions of the Scythian period are in the majority of cases Jaina and Buddhist and if epigraphical evidence is to be relied upon solely for the reconstruction of the history of our sacred literature then we must admit that Brahmanism was not a popular or flourishing religion in Mathurā or the Western part of the United Provinces. The majority of inscriptions discovered in the district of Mathurā and its immediate neighbourhood prove that more than ninety per cent of the sacred edifices in that locality were Buddhist and Jaina from the 1st century B.C. till the 4th century A.D. It is true that one inscription belonging to the year 24 of the reign of Vāṣiṣka records the erection of sacrificial posts for the great *Aśvamedha* sacrifice, but this is a solitary instance. Inscriptions concerning the Orthodox Brahmanical religion or deities are very few in number and indicate that the public patronage of this religion had almost ceased.

With the consolidation of the power of the Imperial Guptas in Northern India the situation changes at once. The majority of records discovered up to date are Brahmanical and not Jaina or Buddhist. It cannot be denied even for a moment that State patronage went to Brāhmaṇas only, though there is no direct evidence to prove this statement. The indirect evidence is to be found in the five Damodarpur and the four Faridpur plates, all of which refer to settlements of land on Hindu gods or Brāhmaṇas.

The attempt of the Brāhmaṇas to re-establish the religion of the Vedic Aryans can be seen from the performance of the *Aśvamedha* by Samudragupta and his grandson Kumāragupta I. The performance of the *Agnihotra* and the five great sacrifices by Brāhmaṇas in the Koṭivarṣa district also indicate the initiation of Vedic sacrifices in the jungle country in Northern Bengal where they were not known before. But Vedic sacrifices no longer appealed to the masses and therefore a very large number of images were carved. The worship of images in India most probably became widespread after the introduction of Northern Buddhism during the rule of the great Kuṣāṇas. How widespread the worship of images had become will be found in a next chapter. The most popular gods were Viṣṇu, Śiva, and Śurya. But forms of these deities with which we are familiar were not so widely diffused as they are now. For example the standing image of Viṣṇu with four hands is rare among Gupta sculptures. We find Viṣṇu either in the form of some of the incarnations or riding on Garuḍa. The later *Avatāras* such as Paraśurāma, Rāmacandra and Balarāma, Buddha and Kalkin are unknown. The most popular *Avatāra* was the Boar (*Varāha*). The Damodarpur plates mention the White Boar *Śveta-Varāha-svāmin*. *Koka-mukha-svāmin* is most probably Śiva and Durgā, as in the case of the Kosam image dedicated in G.E. 139.[1] The phallic emblem of Śiva (*liṅga*) is fairly common. The ordinary modern *liṅga*, which is a cylinder with a round edge top is also known. Such is the *liṅga* dedicated by Pṛthivīṣeṇa, the commander-in-chief of Kumāragupta I at Karamdanda in G.E. 117. The shaft is circular with a round top but the lower part is octagonal and the inscription is incised on this portion. But the *Eka-mukha-liṅga* was more common. In these *liṅgas* there is a human face on the body of the shaft. The later *Caturmukha-liṅga* is rare in the Gupta period. *Eka-mukha-liṅgas* of the Gupta period are very common in Benares city and in the shrine of the *Akṣaya vaṭa* inside Allahabad fort. Such are the magnificent *liṅgas* discovered by the writer at Śaṅkargaḍh and Khoh in the Nagod State of the Baghelkhand Agency of Central India,[2] and the gigantic specimen discovered during the excavation of the Gupta temple found on the plateau of Bhumra in the same State. This *liṅga* is one of the largest known and was discovered inside the sanctum.[3]

The seals discovered by Bloch, Spooner, and

---

1 *Annual Report of the Archæological Survey of India 1913-14, p. 264, Pl. LXX (b.)*

2 *Progress Report of the Archæological Survey of India, Western Circle for the year ending 31st March, 1920, pp. 104-5, Pl. XXVIII-XXIX.*

3 *Ibid., for the year ending 31st March, 1921, pp. 96-7, Pl. XXII (b).*

Marshall at Vaisali and Bhita help us to determine the nature of some of the principal Hindu shrines of the Gupta period. The most important of them still existing is that of the Foot-print of Viṣṇu at Gaya. The Bloch collection contains a magnificent specimen of the seal of the shrine. The upper part bears the mace, an ornamental symbol perhaps a *triśūla,* a conch, a wheel and the symbols of the Sun and the Moon. Among these the mace, conch and the wheel are the special emblems of Viṣṇu. The legend is *Ṣrī-Viṣṇupada-svāmi-Nārāyaṇa.*[1] The seal of the temple of Amrātakeśvara Śiva at Benares comes only second in importance because that shrine is no longer in existence. The seal bears on its upper part a *liṅga* with a *Yoni-paṭṭa* and there is a Triśūla on each side. According to the *Matsya* Purāṇa Amrātakeśvara was one of the eight principal Śaiva shrine of Benares. It was so famous that the Ahom kings of Assam built a temple of Śiva of that name in the village of Ramsa in the Kamrup district.[2] The god is mentioned in a eighteenth century inscription on Kāmākhyā hill in the same district.[3] Spooner found many seals of temples at Vaiśalī but none of them are so important as those mentioned above. Such is the seal of the temple of Rājadharmeśvara in which the emblem is not clear.[4] The seal of

---

1 *Annual Report of the Archæological Survey of India, 1903–4, p 110, No. 31, Pl. XL 3.*

2 *Ibid., pp. 104, 110 ; Pl. XL 2.*

3 *Origin of the Bengali Script, University of Calcutta, 1919, Pl. X.*

4 *Annual Report of the Archaeological Survey of India 1913–14, p. 185 No. 226.*

the temple of Ārāmikīśvara belongs to the Gupta period though Spooner thought it earlier in date. The emblems are a vase, two trees and a combined triśūla and a battle-axe (*paraśu*). At least two specimens were discovered at Vaiśālī but the locality is not known to us.[1] The third seal is unfortunately mutilated but the legend is very interesting as it mentions a *tīrtha* or a holy place.[2] The fourth specimen is far more interesting as it is a seal of a temple of the Sun-god. The upper part is occupied by a fire-altar, which is an emblem characteristic of the connection between fire worship and Sun worship. Spooner saw Iranian influence in this emblem.[3] Marshall found a similar seal at Bhita but there is some difference in the legend. The Vaiśālī seal reads *Bhagavato Adityasya* "(the seal of the temple) of the lord Sun," but the term *Bhagavato* is omitted in the Bhita specimen, which may mean that it is the seal of a person and not a temple.[4] Though Spooner's discussion of the origin of Sun worship is biassed some of his observation are correct. The cult of the Sun has almost disappeared from India now, but the images of that deity, discovered all over India and over long centuries from the first to the twelfth, prove that at one time prior to the Musalman conquest it had a firmer hold on the people of our

---

1 *Ibid., p, 142. Nos. 369, 396 ; Pl. XLVIII.*

2 *Ibid., p. 143, No. 449.*

3 *Ibid., pp. 118–20, 149, No. 607 ; Pl. XLIX.*

4 *Ibid., 1911-12, p. 58, No. 98, Pl. XXI.*

country. Images of the Sun are fairly numerous in the Gupta period and are to be found both as separate images and as decorative figures in *Chaitya*-windows or plaques. These sculptures will be discussed in a subsequent chapter but the seals indicate that the cult of the Sun god was still very popular in the Northern India. This is proved by the popularity of the altar of the Sun, which appear on Sassanian and Scytho-sassanian coinage, and on private seals of the Gupta period. In the Vaiśālī collection of 1903–4 there are at least four seals with this altar. Marshall also discovered four seals at Bhita in 1908–9 with the Fire-altar. Spooner discovered a few in 1913–14 with many different varieties of the altar, the most important of which is No. 607.

Works on Hindu ritual of the Gupta period have not been discovered as yet and therefore it cannot be stated definitely whether the modern Hindu ritual had its origin in this period or not. There seems to be some ground for supposing that the present Hindu ritual was evolved out of the old Vedic ritual during this period.

The revival in and the reform of the Brahmanical or the Hindu religion is also evident from the subdivisions of castes in North-eastern India. Generally speaking castes and sub-castes in the Eastern part of the United Provinces, the North-eastern part of the Central Provinces, the whole of Bihar and Bengal do not correspond to the caste system of the Punjab, Rajputana, or Malwa on the one hand and Gujarat and the Mahārāṣṭra on the other hand. We are not speaking of such provinces of Southern India in which Dravidian languages are still exclusively spoken. In such provinces of Northern, Central, and Western India where Indo-Aryan languages are spoken the caste system can be divided into three great divisions :—

I. The North-eastern castes.

II. The castes of the Punjab and Northern Rajputana.

III. The castes of Southern Rajputana, Malwa, and Northern Gujarat. By the term Northern Gujarat is meant the ancient province of *Uttara-lāṭa* consisting of the Kaḍi *Prānt* of the dominions of the Gaikwad of Baroda, the Māhi-kaṇṭhā States, the Southern part of the Mallāni district of the Jodhpur State and the corresponding portion of the district of Thar and Parkar of Sindh, consisting of the desert *taluqas* of Mithi, Diplo and Nagar-Pārkar. The caste system of British Gujarat, which is *Dakṣiṇa-Lāṭa* is slightly different.

IV. The castes of Southern Gujarat or the districts of Broach and Surat, Northern Konkan consisting of the districts of Thana, Kolaba and Ratnagiri, as well as that of the Mahārāṣṭra.

The difference in the caste system is to be noticed on the following points only :—

I. The absence of a pure Kṣatriya caste and the approximation to it of various royal families.

II. The division of the Vaiśya community into two great groups, the Vaṇika proper with their sub-divisions and a very large number of functional sub-castes who are regarded as Śūdras but are really Vaiśyas.

III. The divisions of Śūdras into three separate groups:—

(i) The higher Śūdras,
(ii) the intermediate Śūdras, and
(iii) the lowest Śūdras and untouchables.

Such differences in the caste system of the Eastern and Western Provinces of Northern India point to one conclusion: that the castes and sub-castes and of the North-eastern Provinces were changed and reclassified long after the last reduction of the *Mānava-Dharma-Śāstra* and these classifications were changed when the Hūṇas conquered the whole of the Western Provinces of Northern India and the West-central districts of Central India. To go deeper into the subject is impossible within the limited compass of this treatise. The castes of Northern Gujarat suffered a second change on account of the obliterating influence of militant Jainism of the period of Hemacandra Sūri and his royal patrons Kumārapāla and Siddharāja Jayasiṁha of Aṇahilapāṭaka. No further changes in the basic rules of the castes of the North-eastern Provinces were needed up to the end of the 12th century, even when the people abandoned Mahāyāna proper and the obscene and revolting rites of Kāla-Cakra-Yāna and Vajrayāna under the Pālas of Bengal.

The gods worshipped, though practically the same as of modern Hindu India were slightly different both in shape and in name. The worship of Viṣṇu was universal as at the present day but the form in favour in the Gupta period was slightly different. Except among the sculptures recently discovered by Mr. K. N. Dikshit M.A. of the Archæological Survey of India, Eastern Circle at Paharpur in the Rajshahi district of Northern Bengal, images of Rādhā and Kṛṣṇa are absolutely unknown in the Gupta period. Even bas-reliefs representing the life of Kṛṣṇa, as described in the 10th *Skandha* of the *Bhāgavata Purāna*, are exceedingly rare. The only specimen known is the huge image unearthed at Sarnath and supposed by Rai Bahadur Pundit Dayaram Sahni as an image of Kṛṣṇa holding the Govardhana mountain, which is a case of mistaken identification.[1] More importance is given to the worship of the Avatāras, "incarnations" of Viṣṇu than to Kṛṣṇa. Among the Avatāras the Boar incarnation appears to have been regarded as more important than any other. The deities mentioned in the Damodarpur plates are Śveta-Varāha-Svāmin and Kokā-Mukha-Svāmin. Śveta-

1 *Not included in the Catalogue of the Museum of Archæology at Sarnath.*

Varāha-Svāmin is undoubtedly the Boar incarnation of Viṣṇu but Kokā-Mukha-Svamin is still unknown. Most probably it was an image of Śiva and Pārvatī. The cave excavated by the Sanikānīka chief, who was the son of the Mahārāja Viṣṇudāsa, contained two images, one of the four-armed Viṣṇu attended by his wives and another of Durgā as Mahiṣa-mardinī.[1] The undated cave inscription of Candragupta II at Udayagiri records the dedication of the cave as a temple of Śiva by one Vīrasena, a hereditary minister. But the Varāha cave, though uninscribed, is distinctly a Vaiṣṇava shrine belonging to the early Gupta period.[2] In the same group at Udayagiri is to be found the colossal image of Viṣṇu lying on the snake-king Ananta twelve feet long.[3] The popularity of the Boar incarnation of Viṣṇu can be gauged from the erection of the great Boar by Mahārāja Dhanyaviṣṇu, the younger brother of the deceased *Mahārāja* Matṛviṣṇu in the first year of the reign of the Hūṇa king Toramāna, which marks the end of the Gupta period proper. In this period two forms of the Boar incarnation were adopted (1) a man with a Boar's head, and (2) a real boar as at Khoh in the Nagod State.[4] Other examples

---

[1] *Gupta Inscriptions, p. 22.*

[2] Cunningham-*Archæological Survey Reports, Vol. X, p. 48-49.*

[3] *Ibid., p. 52.*

[4] *Progress Report of the Archæological Survey of India for the year ending 31st March, 1920, p. 106, pl. XXIX.*

of the incarnations of Viṣṇu, belonging to this period, are to be found at Kaman in the Bharatpur State. There is a fragment bearing the Fish, Tortoise, Boar, Man-Lion and Dwarf incarnations. Most probably the series was complete.[1] The oldest image of the four-armed Viṣṇu is to be found in the Udayagiri cave mentioned above. The next specimen was that the dedication of which was recorded in the inscription of the emperor Skandagupta at Bhitari in the Ghazipur district to which a village was granted.[2] During the reign of the same emperor Cakrapālita, the son of Parṇadatta, the Viceroy of Kathiawad, after the restoration of the great dam of the Sudarśana lake, erected a temple of Viṣṇu and dedicated an image of *Cakrabhṛt*, "the wielder of the Discus."[3] The last example of the dedication of an image of Viṣṇu is that of the colossal image at Eran in the Sagar district of the Central Provinces to which a flag-staff (*Dhvaja-stambha*), was dedicated in the year 165 during the reign of the emperor Budhagupta by the *Mahārāja* Mātṛviṣṇu and his younger brother Dhanyaviṣṇu.[4]

The earliest example of a Śaiva sculpture belonging to the Gupta period has been found at Mathura. The second is the figure of Mahiṣamardinī in the cave at Udayagiri near Sanchi excavated in G.E., 82,[5] with those of the Seven Mothers. The third

---

1 *Ibid.*, *1919, pp. 64–5, pl. XXIV.* 2 *Gupta Inscriptions, pp. 53–56.*

3 *Ibid., pp. 55–56.* 4 *Ibid., pp. 69–90.*

5 Cunningham-*Archæological Survey Report Vol. X, p. 50.*

instance is the temple dedicated by Vīrasena.[1] The fourth instance is the *Liṅga* dedicated under the name of Pṛthivīśvara by Pṛthivīṣeṇa, the minister and commander-in-chief of the emperor Kumāragupta II, which is now preserved in the Lucknow Museum. It is the only known instance of a *Liṅga* belonging to the Gupta period which is neither a natural *Liṅga* nor a *Mukha-liṅgam.*[2] It was dedicated in G.E. 117. The Bilsad pillar inscription of the year 96 mentions the dedication of a temple of Mahāsena or Kārtikeya at Bilsad in the Eta district and this may also be counted among instances of Śaiva temples and images.[3] The *Nāma-liṅgam* mentioned in the fourth Damodārpur plate is the next instance.[4] The most beautiful Śaiva sculptures, with the exception of those discovered at Benares, were found at Kaman, whence they have been removed during recent years to the Ajmer Museum. Such is the great *Caturmmukha-liṅgam* with figures of Viṣṇu, Brahmā, Śiva, and Sūrya on its four sides. The earliest bas-relief representing the marriage of Śiva and Pārvatī discovered in India also came from Kaman to this Museum. The remaining examples of Śaiva sculptures are the *Mukha-liṅgas* discovered by the writer at Khoh and Bhumra in the Nagod State. The Khoh and the Bhumra *Liṅgas* are *Eka-mukha-Liṅgas.* The Khoh speci-

---

1 *Ibid., p. 51–52.* 2 *Epi. Ind., Vol. X, pp. 71–72.*

3 *Gupta Inscriptions, pp. 43–45.*

4 *Epi. Ind., Vol. XV, p. 139.*

men is undoubtedly one of the best specimens of portraiture ever discovered amongst specimens of Gupta art.[1] It is certainly far superior in this respect to the gigantic *Eka-mukha-Liṅga* discovered in the interior of the temple at Bhumra.[2] The use of natural *Liṅgas* appears to have ceased before the beginning of the Gupta period proper, because all *Liṅgas* which can be definitely assigned to the Gupta period are either plain shafts or *Eka-mukha* and *Caturmmukha-Liṅgas.*

After Viṣṇu and Śiva the next important deity in Hinduism of the Gupta period is Sūrya. The worship of this deity has practically disappeared from modern Hinduism and with the exception of solitary shrines in important holy places like Gayā and Benares, temples dedicated to the Sun god are extremely rare. In the Gupta period inscriptions prove the existence of a number of shrines of Sūrya. The earliest record which mentions this deity is the Indor Khera copper plate inscription of the time of the emperor Skandagupta. From this inscription we learn that there was a temple of the Sun at Indrapura, a town in the *Antarvedī* or the Ganges-Jumna *Doab,* built by two Kṣatriyas named Acalavarman and Bhrukuṇṭhasiṁha.[3] There was a great temple of the Sun god in the ancient city of Daśapura in Mālava,

1 *Progress Report of the Archæological Survey of India, Western Circle for the year ending 31st March 1920, pl. XXIX.*

2 *Memoirs of the Archæological Survey of India, No. 16 ; the temple of Siva at Bhumara, pl. XV(c).*

3 *Gupta Inscriptions pp. 70–71.*

modern Mandasor in the Malwa *Prānt* of the dominions of the *Mahārāja* Śinde. During the reign of Kumāragupta I, when *Mahārāja* Bandhuvarman was the Governor of Daśapura, this temple was built by the Guild of silk-weavers from their accumulated wealth. After 36 years, when it had fallen into disrepair, it was rebuilt by the same Guild in V. S., 529=471 A. D.[1] Images of the Sun god are common. The most beautiful example of the representation of the Sun god is to be found in a medallion discovered at Bhumra where the figure is of the type of a Scythian king.[2] It is robed exactly like Kāṇiska[3] as seen in his statue discovered at Mat in the Mathura district. There are no horses in the Bhumra medallion but there are seven such on the *Liṅga* from Kaman in the Ajmer Museum.[4] In this case the Sun god is squatting on his haunches like the unknown Kuṣāṇa statue from Mat.[5] In many cases the forms of Hindu gods and goddesses are totally unlike their present forms. Mahiṣamardinī, now called Durgā, is represented with ten hands at the present day, with eight or twelve in the mediaeval period (800-1200

---

1 *Gupta Inscriptions, pp. 80–87.*

2 *Memoirs of the Archæological Survey of India No. 16, pl. XIV (a).*

3 Coomaraswamy—*History of Indian and Indonesian Art, pl. XVIII, Fig. 65.*

4 *Progress Report of the Archæological Survey of India, Western Circle for the year ending 31st March 1919, pl. XXVI.*

5 Coomaraswamy—*History of Indian and Indonesian Art. pl. XVIII, Fig. 64.*

A. D.), with four hands at Badami [1] in the sixth century, is to be found with the same number of hands in Gupta sculpture proper, *e.g.*, at Bhumra. Similarly in the case of Vaiṣṇava sculptures the image of Viṣṇu seated on the coils of the snake Ananta is to be found at Badami [2] and on the door lintel of the later Gupta temple at Deogadh but no where else in later times. Such images are not worshipped at the present day and very probably became obsolete after the close of the Gupta period.

That Buddhism was flourishing is proved beyond doubt by the great mass of decorative sculpture and number of images discovered at Sarnath alone of all places. There cannot be any doubt about the fact that Sarnath or Buddhist Benares was included in the empire of the early Guptas up to the end of the reign of Bhānugupta. Therefore it cannot be explained for what reasons the Gupta era and the names of most of the Gupta emperors, with the exception of Kumāragupta II and Budhagupta, are omitted in the votive inscriptions of Benares while Candragupta II is mentioned by name and Gupta era is used in the Sanchi inscription of the year 93[3] and the Gupta era used without the name of the reigning emperor Kumāragupta I in the Sanchi inscription of 131.[4] Even the Mankuwar Buddha discovered in the Allahabad

---

1 *Memoirs of the Archæological Survey of India, No. 25, Basreliefs of Badami, pl. II b.*

2 *Ibid., pl. XVII a.*

3 Gupta Inscriptions, *pp. 31–32.*

4 *Ibid., pp. 261–2.*

district mentions Kumāragupta I as the ruling emperor in the year 129.[1]

Jaina inscriptions of the Gupta period betray a certain peculiarity. In the Kahaum pillar inscription of the reign of Skandagupta, the emperor is mentioned by name and the date given in the Gupta era. It records the erection of a stone pillar with five images of the principal Jaina *Tirthankaras* (*Ādi-kartṛs*). In the majority of ancient and mediaeval *Caturmukhas* or *Pratimā-sarvatobhadrikā* only four Jinas are represented. Even on the facets of modern Jaina *Caumuhās* or *Merus* four, eight, and twelve are the usual numbers. Odd numbers, specially five is unknown to Jaina Iconography. Bhagwanlal Indraji suggested that they are the images of Ādinātha, Śāntinātha, Neminātha, Pārśvanātha, and Mahāvīra-Varddhamāna.[2] From the year 135 onwards though the Gupta era is used, votive Buddhist and Jaina inscriptions found in Mathurā do not mention any king, whether Buddhist or Hindu.

A class of terra cotta plaques, so long surmised to be representations of the goddesses of Fertility, Fecundity or the mother goddess, can now be recognised as representations of Śiva and Durgā. The terra cotta plaques in the collection of Major B. D. Basu, I.M.S. (retired) when compared with the stone figure of Śiva and Durgā dedicated

---

[1] *Ibid.*, pp. 46–47. [2] *Gupta Inscriptions*, pp. 66–8.

by Mahārāja Bhīmavarman in G.E., 139 prove the truth of this statement.[1]

Very little was known of the condition of plastic art in ancient Ḍābhāla, mediæval Ḍāhala, Jubbulpur and Rewa in the upper Narmadā-Tons valley. The fortunate discovery of an inscribed image at Dhuan Dhar near the falls of the Narmadā at Bhera Ghat or the Marble Rocks has proved that in the 2nd century A.D., plastic art was yet in its nascent stage. One such image was introduced in later times into the circular temple of the Sixty-four Yoginīs. This temple contains images of three different dates of which the inscribed images, described by me in my memoir on the Haihayas of Tripurī and their monuments, were dedicated by queen Nohalā, wife of Lakṣmaṇarāja.[2] Earlier than these there are several images in this circular temple all of which are standing and uninscribed.[3] These images evidently belong to the Gupta period, when the Parivrājaka *Mahārājas* and the chiefs of Ucchakalpa ruled over the country between the rivers Tons and Narmadā. The evolution of the human figure in this country, as evidenced by the Dhuan Dhar images discovered by the late Mr. H. Panday and the 10th century images of the Cedī period, would point out that the intermediate images must belong to the Gupta period.

---

1 *Annual Report of the Archæological Survey of India 1913-14, pp. 262-4 ; pl. LXXb-c.*

2 *Memoirs of the Archæological Survey of India, No. 23, pp. 79–91.*

3 *Ibid., p. 86, Nos. 49–52.*

CHAPTER IV.

ARCHITECTURE.

Specimens of civil and domestic architecture of the period are still very rare, in spite of the excavations carried on by the Indian Archæological Department at Rājagṛiha, Pātaliputra, Vaiśālī, Benares, Bhiṭā, Kosām, and Kurukṣetra. Marshall's dating of the buildings at Bhiṭā is very appealing but totally unscientific. The assignment of such early dates to a building simply because a single seal or stone-axe was found in a chamber is unconvincing. The amount of material discovered by the late Drs. Bloch and Spooner at Vaiśālī prove that the chamber in which the seals were discovered belong to the Gupta period along with the connected buildings of the same series and stratum, but nothing is left of such buildings today and even the bricks of the walls excavated have been carried away. Similarly, the Gupta structures discovered by Spooner in the uppermost stratum of his excavations at Pāṭaliputra have also disappeared. Even when they were just unearthed they conveyed very little to the student of the history of our architecture.

There remains to be discussed the architecture of the sacred buildings of the period of which a few examples have survived up to our times.

Even at the pre. lar decorative m is considerable divergence of opinion amongst scholars regarding the true type of temples of Gupta period proper. Earlier writers were of opinion that like most modern and mediaeval temples, temples of the Gupta type also possessed *Śikharas* or spires. The most prominent examples cited by Cunningham and other earlier writers are the great brick temples at Bhitargaon in the Cawnpore district and Mahābodhi or Bodh-gaya in the Gaya district. The same class of writers described other Gupta temples, *e.g.*, those at Sanchi, Tigowa in the Jubbulpur district and at Bodh-Gaya as being flat-roofed. Recent discoveries of Gupta temples have proved that the Gupta temple proper did not possess a *Śikhara*. In the case of the Mahābodhi temple at Bodh-Gaya the arguments produced for assigning it to the Gupta period are: that it was seen by the Chinese pilgrim Yuan Chwang, that the dimensions [1] given by him agree with those of the present temple before its repairs, that the Ceylonese king Meghavarṇa sent an embassy to Samudragupta asking for a permission to build a monastery at Bodh-Gaya [2], and finally the Chinese pilgrim I-Tsing states that the Mahābodhi *Vihāra* was built by the Ceylonese. Chavannes has proved from Chinese records that the Mahābodhi *Vihāra* was built by a king of Ceylon. "Near the Bodhi tree was the Mahābodhi

---

[1] Coomaraswamy—*History of Indian and Indonesian Art, p. 81.*

[2] Smith—*Early History of India, 4th Edition, p. 304.*

Vihāra built by a king of Ceylon."[1] Writers like Mr. E. B. Havell think tnat the Mahābodhi temple was built in the first century B.C.[2] After a thorough examination of the entire structure of the Mahābodhi temple the writer could find no trace, both inside and outside, of decorative *motifs* of the Gupta period in any part of it. On the other hand all other temples whether Buddhist or Hindu, which can be definitely assigned to the Gupta period on the ground of epigraphy, always show the use of decorative *motifs* distinctive of the Gupta period, *e.g.*, the original main Shrine and the Gupta monasteries at Sarnath, the Hindu temple at Muṇḍeśvarī near Bhabua in the Arrah district, the Gupta temple at Bodh-Gaya, the temple of Pārvatī at Nachna-Kuthara in the Ajaygadh State, the temple of Śiva at Bhumara in the Nagod State, the later Gupta temple at Deogadh in the Jhansi district and the Gupta temple at Sanchi in the Bhopal State.

The original outline of the Mahābodhi temple was of a different shape, which was changed when it was encased in fresh masonry at the time of its repairs (1880–92). This slim outline of the *Śikhara* can be seen in earlier photographs.[3] The outline of the original *Śikhara* along with the

---

[1] Takakusu—*I-Tsing, quoting Chavannes, Memoirs, p. 84; p. xxxii and Note 2.*

[2] *A Study of Indo-Aryan Civilisation, p. 100.*

[3] R. L. Mitra—*Buddha-Gaya, pl. XV;* Cunningham—*Mahabodhi, pl. XXXI.*

absence of particular decorative *motifs* of the Gupta period proper prove that the Mahābodhi temple could not have been erected earlier than the 8th century A.D. There are two other temples of the same type and probably of the same date in South Bihar, one of which, though not repaired, is still in better preservation than the original Mahābodhi temple. These are the temple of Śiva at Konch, near Tikari, in the Gaya district and the great Buddhist *Vihāra* at Nālandā in the Patna district. The latter was excavated and partly destroyed by the late Mr. A. M. Broadley, I.C.S., when most of the carved stones were removed to the Museum unded by him at Bihar whence they were removed o the Calcutta Museum in 1897-98. The ruins have been re-excavated recently by the Archæological Survey of India. In this temple the *Śikhara* collapsed long ago. According to an inscription discovered on the door-jamb of this temple it was rebuilt in the 11th year of the reign of Mahīpāla I of Bengal *i.e.*, towards the close of the 10th century A.D. The *motifs* employed here and at Konch prove that the present Mahābodhi temple can not be earlier than the 8th century A.D.

The great brick temple at Bhitargaon in the Cawnpore district lies twenty miles to the south of Cawnpore town. The temple was first described by Cunningham in 1875-76 and he assigned it to the Gupta period.[1] It was more

---

[1] *Archæological Survey Reports Vol. XI, pp. 40-46.*

accurately surveyed in recent times by Dr. J. Ph. Vogel, formerly a Superintendent of the Archæological Survey of India. Dr. Vogel states, "The outer ornamentation of terra cotta sculpture is certainly the most striking feature of the Bhitargaon temple (Plates IV and V). The walls rise in bold mouldings, their upper portions being decorated with a row of rectangular panels alternating with ornamental pilasters. It has been noticed above that the early plinth of the Nirvāṇa temple at Kasia is embellished in a very similar fashion and that on that account there is good reason to ascribe the Bhitargaon temple to the early Gupta period."[1] The exterior walls of this temple were decorated with terra cotta panels in niches, proving that it did not belong to the type of the sancta at Bhumara or Nachna Kuthara. Moreover, there is a *Śikhara* in which there is a series of arches which are not exactly *Caitya*-windows.[2] The plinth mouldings are totally absent proving the difference between it and the temples at Nachna Kuthara and Bhumara.[3] Therefore, its affinity lies more with the temple at Deogadh than with those of Nachna Kuthara and Bhumara because of the presence of the stumpy *Śikhara*.[4] The art of the terra cotta panels of the Bhitargaon temple have been assigned

---

1 *Annual Report of the Archæological Survey of India, 1908-9, p. 9,*

2 *Ibid., pl. I.*

3 *Memoirs of the Archæological Survey of India, No. 16. pl. II.*

4 Cunningham—*Archæological Survey Report, Vol. XI. pl. XV.*

to the Gupta period without sufficient reasons. A closer comparison with the products of the three great schools of Gupta Art in India e.g., Mathurā, Benares, and Pāṭaliputra prove that the terra cotta panels of Bhitargaon are later in date than the great Deogadh panels or the finer bas-reliefs of Sarnath. The mediaeval art of the United Provinces still remains to be studied. Sufficient remains of the periods of Bhoja I, Adivāraha and his son Mahendrapāla I, have been discovered all over the United Provinces but these scattered remains have not been analysed yet. Inscribed records of Bhoja I [1] on sculpture exist at Deogadh and Pehoa and some of Mahīpāla I at Asni in the Fatehpur district. At the same time the *Śikhara* of the Bhitargaon temple and its decorative *motifs* bear a curious resemblance to those of the temple of the Somavaṁśī kings in the Raipur district of the Central Provinces.[2]

The temples of the early, later and post-Gupta periods are enumerated below:—

I. Early Gupta (319–550 A.D.):—

1. The temple of Śiva at Bhumra, about six miles from Unchehra railway station on Jubbulpur-Itarsi Section of the G.I.P. Ry., discovered by the writer in 1920.

---

1 *Ibid., Vol. X, pl. XXXIII.*

2 *Ibid., Vol. XVII, pl. XVI*; E. B. Havell—*A Study of Indo-Aryan Civilization pl. XXXV, L, and LI.*

2. The earlier temple of Śiva at Nachna Kuthara, called temple of Pārvatī by Cunningham, in the Ajaygadh state, about 10 miles from Bhumra, described by Cunningham and by the writer in 1919.
3. The temple called "Lad Khan's temple" at Aihole in the Bijapur district of the Bombay Presidency, built in the Early Cālukya times.

II. Later Gupta (551-605 A.D.):—

4. The later Gupta temple at Deogadh in Jhansi district, generally mistaken to be an Early Gupta structure.

III. Post-Gupta (606-700 A.D.):—

5. The small Post-Gupta temple at Śaṅkargadh in the Nagod State, discovered by the writer in 1920.
6. The Post-Gupta temple at Nachna Kuthara in the Ajaygadh district, discovered by Cunningham and described by the writer in 1919.
7. The Post-Gupta temple at Muṇḍeśvarī, near Bhabua in the Arrah or Shahabad district of Bihar and Orissa.

Though no large inscription has been discovered in the temples at Deogadh, Bhumra, and Nachna Kuthara, the dates of these three temples can be accurately deduced from short inscriptions and mason's marks. From these data we can safely deduce that the flat-roofed temples of Bhumra and Nachna Kuthara belong to the Early Gupta period, which ended in the middle of the 6th century A.D. These two temples must be described before considering the Later and Post-Gupta temples.

In the case of both of these temples the architect was concerned more with the provision of a covered path of circumambulation (*pradaksiṇā-patha*) as at Elephanta, than with a *Śikhara*. In fact, though there is a small chamber above the main shrine in the case of the Early Gupta temple at Nachna Kuthara, there is no indication of any *Śikhāra* in the case of both of these structures. In both cases the flat roof of the sanctum or the chamber above it indicates that there was no *Śikhara.* The earlier temple at Nachna Kuthara possesses a small flat-roofed chamber above the sanctum, proving thereby that the architect did not intend to build a *Śikhara* over this shrine. These two temples prove that the origin of the *Śikhara* or spire in Indian temple architecture is much later than the period of domination of the Early Gupta Emperors in Northern India. From its style as well as the mason's marks in the temple of Śiva discovered at Bhumra, this one is the earlier of the two. The remains of this shrine were excavated by the writer in 1920-21. The entire shrine was 35′ square. In front of this square area was the plinth of the *Maṇḍapa* or porch measuring 29′-10″ by 13′. There is a flight of steps in front of this porch, on each side of which were discovered the plinths of two smaller shrines, measuring 8′—2″ by 5′—8″. In the centre of the square portion of the plinth is the sanctum or *Garbha-gṛha*, measuring 15′—6″ square, built of finely dressed Kaimur red sandstone without any mortar and roofed with long flat slabs. The rest of the space in the square area, which enclosed the sanctum, was a covered path of circumambulation as can be proved from the analogy of the exactly similar existing structures at Nachna Kuthara and Aihole, which are lighted by stone-windows of pierced screens on the sides.

The earlier temple at Nachna Kuthara is practically of the same size as that at Bhumra. The sanctum in this case measures 15′—6″ on the outside and 8′ inside. The larger chamber, or path of circumambulation, which encloses the sanctum is 33′ on the outside and 26′ in the interior. The *Maṇḍapa* in this case measures 26′ by 12′. The steps at Nachna Kuthara are 18′ by 10′ while those at Bhumara are 11′—3″ by 8′—5″. The masonry in the case of both temples is finely coursed ashlar. The difference between these two temples lies in the detailed and exceedingly fine decorations of the Bhumra temple compared with which that at Nachna Kuthara is much plainer. While the path of circumambulation and the porch of the Bhumra temple are completely ruined, the entire structure at Nachna Kuthara was in a much better state of preservation in 1919. There is another point of difference between these two temples, which is the absence of any structure over the sanctum in the case of the temple at Bhumra. The only example of a flat roofed shrine surrounded by a covered path of circumambulation in which there is no structure over the sanctum, the temple at Bhumra, is unique in this respect. Coomaraswamy places the temple of Lad Khan at Aihole, without sufficient reason in *circa* 450 A.D. Beyond the resemblance with the earlier temple at Nachna Kuthara in having a small square cell above the sanctum and a covered path of circumambulation around the latter, lighted by large windows of pierced screens, there is no other reason to place the date of the erection of this temple earlier than the time of Kīrttivarman I of Badami, *i.e.*, the first half of the 6th century A.D.

The Early Gupta Temple was therefore, in type, a flat roofed sanctum, with a covered path for circumambulation, having an open porch in front decorated with pure Gupta *motifs*. It is not possible for us to determine how this type came to be copied in the 6th century A.D., at Badami; but the designs survived in the Malabar country up to the end of the 16th century. On the Malabar coast, especially in the modern districts of North and South Kanara, square shrines, surrounded by one or more covered paths of circumambulation, have been discovered in very large numbers, from Mudabidri near Mangalore to Gersoppa and Bhatkal in the north. In the case of all of these temples, there is no *Śikhara* over the sanctum, but the excessive rainfall of the districts demanded that the slab-roof should be sloping instead of being flat. Hence the roofs of the sancta as well as the single or double paths of circumambulation are made of stone slabs, placed in a slanting position like tiled roofs of modern buildings. This particular type of temples resembles the Early Gupta Type in many particulars; *e.g.*, the want of a *Śikhara*, one or more covered paths of circumambulation, a small open porch in the centre of the *façade* and want of ornamentations on the exterior. These temples in the north and south Kanara district are Hindu and Jaina. The Jain temples are called *Bastis* and some of them contain big and elaborate establishments. The general decline of Jainism along the Malabar coast has caused the desertion of many of these *Bastis*, but due to the munificence of the Vijayanagara emperors and the chiefs of Sugandhā or Sonda, the majority of Hindu temples are in a much better state of preservation, comparatively. The example of the great Jaina *Basti* at Bhatkal in the extreme south of the North Kanara district of the Bombay Presidency may be cited. In this case the roof of the sanctum, the path of circumambulation and the porch are all sloping and constructed of long thick plain slabs of stone finely dove-tailed and placed on heavy stone beams. The exterior is severely plain but the interior shows an amazing mass of decorative carving of the south Indian type which is quite different from the decadent Hoyśala *motifs* of Hampe, Penukonda, Chandragiri and Udayagiri. Another feature of these Malabar temples is that in the majority of cases they are built on stone piles, having empty spaces under the floors. There is a lamp post (*dīpa-stambha*) in each of them, which is a monolithic pillar surmounted by a stone lantern, standing apart from the building. The sloping roofs of the Jaina *Basti* of Bhatkal decrease gradually in height; the roof of the sanctum being the highest, next to it comes that of the first path of circumambulation, then comes the second path of cirumambulation, while that of the porch is the lowest. It is impossible at the present day to find out how the Early Gupta-Temple-type came to survive in a modified form in the extreme south-west of the Indian peninsula and survived there for eleven centuries after the Gupta period. Some links have been discovered recently in the country between East Central India and the Malabar Coast. Though these links possess *Śikharas*, their plan consists of a small *Garbha-gṛha* enclosed by a covered path of circumambulation. Such are the temples of Samgameśvara, Mallikārjuna [1] and Virupāksha [2] at Pattadkal in the Bijapur district of the Bombay Presi-

---

1 Cousens—*Chalukyan Architecture of the Kanarese districts, pl.* XXXV.

2 *Ibid, pl. XLV.*

dency. A similar arrangement exists in the Meguti temple [1], the Huchchimalli-gudi [2], temple No. 9 [3] at Aihole and in the two temples at Mahākūṭa [4] in the same district. The second link is to be found in the group of Chandella temples at Khajuraho in the Chhattarpur State near Nowgong, slightly S.S.W. of Bhumra and Nachna Kuthara. In the Khajuraho temples, in one or two cases, a small passage has been left between the *Garbha-gṛha* and the three *Ardha-maṇḍapas* on three sides of it.

Out of the two early Gupta temples, the one at Nachna Kuthara was in a better state of preservation and from its analogy we can guess that the path of circumambulation at Bhumra also was devoid of detailed ornamentation in the interior. The exterior in this case also may have been ornamented and the slabs discovered during the excavations, consisting of sunkel panels divided by pilasters, with figures of *gaṇas* or goblins alternately, may have formed the exterior decoration.[5] The very great number of ornamental sculptures discovered during the excavation of the temple at Bhumra proves that the *Maṇḍapa* at that place was much more elaborately decorated than the existing porch at Nachna Kuthara. This *Maṇḍapa* possessed at least one finely decorated gateway.

---

1 *Ibid., pl. IV.* 2 *Ibid., pl. XIII.*

3 *Ibid., pl. XVI.* 4 *Ibid., pl. XXVII.*

5 *Memoirs of the Archæological Survey of India, No. 16; the Temple of Śiva at Bhumra, pp. 8–10; pl. IX–XI.*

Four fragments of this gateway were recovered and on them we see the shaft of a pilaster, shaped like the rough bark of the date-palm. A parallel band bears on it that exquisitely fine arabesque which is characteristic of pure Gupta work. Miniature dwarfs are turning somersaults at the corners of the bases of the pilasters.[1] The roof of the interior of the porch was supported by graceful tapering pillars, embedded in foliated vases, the shafts of some of which are plain and some fluted.[2] Set against the plain ashlar masonry of the inner wall of the path of circum-ambulation and the sanctum were numerous pilasters with plain or octagonal shafts but ornamented with square bosses bearing some of the finest arabesque medallions, ever discovered in India, as well as *Kīrtimukhas*.[3] The zenith of artistic excellence is reached in the case of the ornate slabs of the flat roof, many of which were recovered in a wonderful state of preservation. One of them bears on its surface a mass of arabesque foliage with a long stem, clinging to it are superb little *Amorini*; on the other we see a giant creeper with huge corrugated leaves reminiscent of Acanthus leaves of Corinthian architecture; and on a third the representations of huge waves with breaking crests.[4] These roofing slabs are of different sizes and on others, which are narrower, we find arabesque which is

[1] *Ibid., pl. IV.*
[2] *Ibid., pl. VI.*
[3] *Ibid., pl. V.*
[4] *Ibid, pl. VII.*

relatively mediocre compared with the three described above. There are others in which leaves are arranged in squares as well as geometrical patterns.[1] Very probably the porch of *Maṇḍapa* was open on three sides and the lower part of its sides was composed of decorated slabs. The exterior of the porch was decorated with a line of indescribably fine *Caitya*-windows, containing round medallions with figures of Hindu gods and goddesses. These *Caitya*-windows can be crossly divided into four classes; (a) according to size and (b) according to ornamentation. Larger and smaller *Caitya*-windows were probably placed alternately along the cornice. The larger *Caitya*-windows are ornamented along the circumference of the medallions either with (i) arabesque or (ii) two small lotuses.[2] The medallions contain figures of Gaṇeśa, Brahmā, Yama, Kubera, Kārtikeya, Śiva dancing, Śiva seated on his bull, Sūrya, Devī as Mahisha-mardinī and Kāma. In one or two cases the smaller *Caitya*-windows contain either small figures of dancing *Amorini* or full lotus rosettes. From analogy it appears that such *Caitya*-windows were placed alternately according to size. Such is the position of these decorative figures on the cornice of the so-called Dharmarāja's ratha at Mamallapuram in the Chingleput district of the Madras Presidency.[3] Exactly similar but

---

1 *Ibid., pl. VIII.* 2 *Ibid., pls. XII—XIV.*

3 Havell—*A Study of Indo-Aryan civilization. The ancient and mediaeval architecture of India. London, 1915, p. 87, fig. 36.*

smaller *Caitya*-windows have been discovered in the early Gupta temple at Nachna Kuthara.[1]

The masonry of both of the early Gupta temples is finely coursed small ashlar. The architect did not provide for the extremes of expansion and consequently all stones of the surface are either badly cracked or chipped at the corners, a characteristic to be found in the Daśāvatāra temple at Deogadh in the Jhansi District, the unfinished temple on the mound at Nemawar, on the Narmadā, in the Indore State[2] and in the Śaiva monastery at Chandrehe in the Rewa State.[3] No mortar has been used in the construction of any of these two temples, nor was clamping resorted to. There was no great weight upon the walls and pillars of these two temples as the height was not much and the roofs all flat. The collapse of these two temples is due entirely to the cracking of the lintels and displacement of the foundations by tropical vegetation.

Towards the close of the 6th century A.D., a new member was added to the top of the flat roof of the sanctum. This was the beginning of the *Sikhara* in Northern India. The earliest example of this new member in Indian Architecture is to be found in the later Gupta temple at Deogadh

---

[1] Cunningham—*Archæological Survey Reports, Vol. XXI, pl. XXVI.*

[2] *Progress Report of the Archæological Survey of India, Western Circle, for the year ending 31st March, 1921, pp. 102–6, pl. XXVII.*

[3] *Ibid., pp. 83—5, pl. XIV.*

10

in the Jhansi district. The photograph published by Cunningham in 1875 shows the remains of this new member, decorated with *Caitya*-windows and other distinctly Gupta decorative *motifs*.[1] Other temples of the same period are those discovered by the present writer at Sankargadh,[2] in the Nagod State and by Cunningham at Nachna Kuthara,[3] in the Ajaygadh State. The temple at Śankargadh is earlier than the later temple at Nachna Kuthara. The date of this small temple can be fixed by a comparison of its carved door-frame with that in the later Gupta temple at Deogadh. During a recent visit to Deogadh the writer found that the plinth of the Daśāvatāra temple has been fully excavated. The plan of the temple is slightly different from that given by Cunningham. It is now certain that in this temple also there was a covered path of circumambulation, one beam of which is still sticking out; but there were four entrances to it instead of one, and all of them were provided with small porches and staircases. There were four small temples at the four corners which were probably capped by small *Āmalakas*, many of which were discovered during the excavations. On each side of each of the staircases there was a niche, only one of which is nearly entire.

---

1 Cunningham—*Archæological Survey Reports, Vol. X, pl. XXXV.*

2 *Progress Report of the Archæological Survey of India, Western Circle, for the year ending 31st March, 1920, pp. 104-5, pl. XXVII.*

3 *Ibid., 1919, p. 61, pl. XVII.*

Surrounding the main temple there were a number of smaller shrines, the plinth levels of which are much lower than that of the Daśāvatāra temple. But they appear to be of a later date from some carving on some of them. One of them bears on it a row of square rosettes, placed alternately between inverted stepped pyramids, a design too common in the mediæval Jain temples on the top of the hill at Deogadh. The excavation of the area surrounding the Daśāvatāra temple has revealed many interesting facts unknown to Cunningham and earlier writers. The first is that of large pillars with the regular Gupta decorative *motifs* of half and three-quarters medallions on the shaft and foliated vases at the top or the bottom. Several such have been discovered, it appears at different times, but the one which lies by the side of the new sculpture-shed nearest to the Daśāvatāra temple bears on it a longish inscription in two lines in characters of the late sixth century. Evidently such pillars were used in the four porches and the temple cannot be much earlier than 575 A.D. Another interesting feature discovered during the recent excavations is the presence of a number of vignettes in the medallions of *Caitya*-windows. One of them is very clearly a vignette within another, while the second shows a door-way or niche within a vignette. The number of *Caitya*-windows discovered prove the truth of the author's previous theories about the employment of these members in the flat-roofed temples of Bhumra and Nachna Kuthara. In addition to the figures inside the medallions discovered at these two places, the new Deogadh-finds include the well-known Sarnath *motif,* of twin columns with cruciform capitals inside the medallions of Caitya-windows.[1]

The importance of the Deogadh temple lies in its *Śikhara.* The *Śikhara* of the Daśāvatāra temple is low with gradual curves in it as in the case of the temples of Paraśurāmeśvara and Mukteśvara at Bhuvaneśvara, the twin temples at Gandharāḍi in the Baudh State and a number of Early Cālukyan temples at Aihoḷe and Pattadkal in the Bijapur district of the Bombay Presidency. Only the lower portion of the *Śikhara* of the Daśāvatāra temple remains, but the entire contour can be judged and determined from it. Surrounding the base of this low pyramidal *Śikhara* was the flat roof of the path of circumambulation, the edge of which was decorated with large and small *Caitya*-windows with medallions as are to be found on the edge of the free-standing *rathas* at Mamallapuram in the Chingleput district. Two large pillars stood in the centre of each facade, supporting the porch and on its sides rose a short wall, on which were placed dwarf pillars and pilasters supporting the flat roof. Against each of these two walls on the sides of each

---

1 D. R. Sahni, *Catalogue of the Museum of Archæology at Sarnath*, pp. 254–58.

porch rose in relief a slender but fairly tall niche containing some divine figure. Above the line of the topmost plinth-moulding were used large thick slabs of stone bearing stumpy pilasters alternated with figures of *gaṇas*. The smaller temples in the four corners most probably contained the *bassi relievi* discovered in previous years.[1]

In the remaining portions of the *Śikhara*, the decorative *motif* predominating, is the *Caitya*-window. They were, however, much more distinct in Cunningham's time than at the present day. This is the beginning of the long history of this *motif* which became unrecognisable in its later stylized form.

In its front facade the entrance to the sanctum is fitted with a door-frame of the same style as those at Bhumra and Nachna Kuthara. We find the same divine figures, larger in number, at the bottoms of the door-jambs, which consist of more than one upright; the continuation of some of the arabesques and superimposed panels on the lintel, the false extension of the sides of the lintel to give an idea of massivity and finally the addition of a large boss in the centre of the lower part of the lintel bearing a fine bas-relief. In the Śiva temple at Bhumra this boss bears in relief a fine bust of Śiva, the place of which is taken in the Daśavatāra temple by a small figure of Nārāyaṇa

[1] Coomaraswamy, *History of Art in India and Indonesia, pl. XLIV, fig. 167.*

seated on the coils of Ananta or Śeṣa. The representation of Viṣṇu of this particular style are extremely rare and no other specimen is known to us in Northern India. The only other specimen known to the writer is to be found in the great Vaiṣṇava cave-temple (No. IV) at Badami in the Bijapur district of the Bombay Presidency.[1]

The Daśāvatāra temple presents another new feature in its arrangement and decorative details of the three great niches containing the great bas-reliefs. Here we see for the first time the familiar Gupta *motifs* in actual use. Each niche is contained in a sunken panel formed by two uprights and a horizontal beam but most of the decorations, in all cases, go above this beam. In the case of the upright, the decorations running parallel to them, are continued in the interior but not outside. These uprights are pilasters of the familiar Gupta type ; square at the bottom, plain in the lower half, bearing a narrow band of arabesque on an elevation at the bottom and the centre. In the upper half ornaments are more profuse and beginning with the three-quarters medallion containing a bas-relief it ends with a dwarf-foliated vase bearing a square abacus. Above this is a cruciform capital, partly Indo-Persepolitan in style, as below each arm one can see lions couchant in the approved and well-known method. The medallions of the pilasters contain

[1] *Memoirs of the Archæological Survey of India*, No. 25, *pl.* XVII *a.*

in the case of the niche containing the great Śeṣa-śāyin, a four armed Ganeśa seated on the left and a two-armed figure on the right. Inside the area enclosed by these two pilasters there are two more uprights, a pair against each pilaster, both of which bear arabesque in the interspaces of meandering creepers, which is continued in the two lower bars of the lintel. A third bar is interposed below the real lintel, supported on cruciform capitals, and in this case also, the ornament is slightly variegated arabesque. On the great lintel itself, we see one of those extremely nimble artistic ideas executed in stone, consisting of a creeper with foliage, entirely unnatural, but which, somehow or other, looks very natural, with playful *Amorini* in the centre. Above the real lintel rises another tier with alternated sunken panels. It looks, from a distance, as if short uprights have been placed on the horizontal beam to support the sloping roof of a temple. The sunken panels bear niches or doorways carved in very shallow relief and the surface ones real lion's heads or *Kīrttimukhas.* The sloping roof above is of the same shape as the *Maṇḍapas* (*Jagamohanas*) of early mediæval Orissan temples like the Paraśurāmeśvara [1] at Bhuvaneśvara or the twin temples at Gandharāḍi [2] in the Baudh State. A row of small dentils appear below the roof but over it

1 Monmohan Ganguly, *Orissa and her remains ancient and mediæval. pl. XII.*

2 *Journal of the Bihar & Orissa Research Society, Vol. XV, pp. 73–80 pl. I–II.*

is continued one of the principal architraves of the temple. It is brought over the roof of each of the niches by two advancing recessed corners. The ornamentations consist of a row of sunken panels, oblong in shape, containing niches in miniature and separated from each other by a number of flat pilasters bearing either, three long pilasters, or a mass of arabesque resembling small Acanthus leaves.

The ornamentation of the niches on the three sides of the Daśāvatāra temple differs and it is apparent that the temple must have been thoroughly repaired sometime in the 7th or 8th century A.D. It is in these later additions that a definite connection can be traced between the early Gupta decorative style of niches and the slightly later Gurjjara-Pratīhāra style, a very good example of which was found by Pundit Govind Mālaviya to the proper right of the great Jaina temple on the low hill to the west of the Daśāvatāra temple.[1] The original idea underlying the addition of this new member over the flat roof of the sanctum must have been to accentuate or emphasize the position of the sanctum and to distinguish it from the rest of the structure. The corners of the *Śikharas* of the temples at Deogadh and Sankargadh show a slight curvature, which is to be found in the earliest mediæval temples of Orissa; in the Paraśurāmesvara temple at Bhuvaneśvara

[1] Cunningham—*Archæological Survey Reports, Vol. X, pl. XXIV.*

and the twin temples at Gandharāḍi in the Baudh State. In these the height of the *Śikhara* from the point of its junction with the side walls is exactly one-and-a-half of the side walls. Unaccountably the same proportion is to be observed in the brick temples at Sirpur, in the Central Provinces which do not belong to the 6th century as Coomaraswamy[1] supposes but to the 8th century according to the Sirpur inscription of the Somavaṁśī kings.[2] The *Śikhara* became a regular feature of Indian temples from the beginning of the 7th century A.D., though even so late as the 10th, an upper chamber continued to be erected in certain cases; such as the one on the top of the sanctum of the Buddhist temple (No. 45) at Sanchi.[3]

There are a number of temples, also belonging to the Gupta period, which are generally taken to represent the type of temples of this period, because they were the earliest to be discovered. Such are the small temples of Bodh-Gaya, in the Gaya district, Tigowa, in the Jubbulpur district, and Sanchi, in the Bhopal State. These temples consist of a square sanctum with a small porch or verandah in front of it. The temple at Tigowa is probably earlier in date than the Gupta period proper, because the pillars and pilasters of the verandah bear Indo-Persepolitan capitals. The

---

1 *A History of Art in Indica, and Indonesia, pl. LI, Fig. 186.*

2 *Epigraphia Indica, Vol. XI, pp. 184–97.*

3 *Annual Report of the Archæological Survey of India, 1913–14, Part II, pl. XXII.*

size of the small temples at Sanchi and Bodh-Gaya prove that they were auxiliary temples and not principal shrines. But because they were the earliest known temples of the Gupta period, they came to be called the representative type of temples of the Gupta period. Recent discoveries have proved that the Gupta temple at Bodh-Gaya, to the right of the passage as one gets out of the doorway of the Great Temple, is perhaps the same as that built by the Ceylonese. The Gupta temples at Sanchi and Bodh-Gaya are Buddhist temples or shrines, the type of which had just lost its originality, because at this stage both Buddhist and Jain temples were beginning to be unified with the Hindu or Brahmanical temple type.

The oldest known temples of Northern India, belonging to the earlier part of the 7th century A.D., are the second temple at Nachna Kuthara and the temple of Mundeśvarī, near Bhabua, in the Shahabad or Arrah district of Bihar and Orissa. At Nachna Kuthara the second temple possesses a fine *Śikhara*. It lies to the south-west of the early Gupta Temple and enshrines one of the largest four-faced *Liṅgas* (*Caturmukha-Mahādeva*) ever discovered. In front of the sanctum there was a small porch of twelve pillars which had collapsed when the present writer saw it in 1919. The sanctum is a plain square cell without an *Antarāla*, on the top of which is a modest *Śikhara*. The upper part of the *Śikhara*, consisting of the pinnacle, is damaged. From a distance this temple looks like other temples of the mediæval period of Northern India (800–1200 A.D.), but a closer scrutiny reveals certain features, which tend to prove that this temple must be very closely allied in date to the fifth and sixth century temples described in the preceding pages. The most important feature is the door-frame. The resemblance of the plastic work and the arrangement of its door-frame to that at Bhumra is so complete that it is extremely difficult to believe that they are even slightly different in date. The arabesque of the first band with the climbing *Amorini*, the flying figures of the lintel and the false recesses at the ends of the lintel containing female figures all point out to a contiguous building period and not a distant one. There was no path of circumambulation in this case and the exterior of the walls of the sanctum are perfectly finished and decorated with small niches. The stone door-frame of the sanctum is one of the very rare examples of 7th century art discovered up-to-date in Northern India. The presence of the river goddesses, Gaṅgā and Yamunā, in the case of the early Gupta temples at Bhumra, Besnagar,[1] Deogadh[2] and the earlier temple at the same place show that it was a constant feature in Gupta architecture proper. But these figures are absent at

---

1 Coomaraswamy—*History of Art in India and Indonesia, pl. XLVII, fig. 177.*

2 Cunningham—*Archæological Survey Reports, Vol. X, pl. XXXVI.*

the bottom of the jambs of the post-Gupta temple at Nachna Kuthara, though they are present in the Mundésvarī temple. The stone door-frame of the 8th century temples at Dhamtari and Sirpur in the Central Provinces are slightly different from that of the post-Gupta temple of Nachna Kuthara.

The temple of Mundeśverī, discovered by the late Dr. T. Bloch in 1905-6, has not drawn that amount of attention, which it deserves. It was actually in existence in the Harṣa year 30=635-6 A.D. The only person who has mentioned it in the history of architecture is Coomarswamy; but even he has omitted to publish its photograph at the time of its discovery. Bloch discovered fragments of a votive inscription one section of which was discovered by the late Mr. P. C. Mukharji as early as 1891. This inscription was inscribed on a separate pillar and records a donation by a noble named Bhāgudalana in the reign of a minor prince named Udayasena, who held the titles of *Mahāsāmanta*, *Mahāpratīhara*, and *Mahārāja* and who was evidently a subordinate chief under Harṣa. This inscription mentions the erection of a temple (*Maṭha*) close to the temple of Vinīteśvara and certain donations to a temple of Viṣṇu called Maṇḍaleśvara. The present name Muṇḍeśvarī is evidently a corruption of the ancient Maṇḍaleśvara.[1] This temple underwent consider-

---

[1] *Epigraphia Indica, Vol. IX, pp. 282-3.*

able changes during the Pāla period (800–1200 A.D.) when many additions and alterations were carried out. Though the *Śikhara* has disappeared and in the place of the large smooth ashlar work the Public Works Department of the British Government has crowned it with a low parapet of undressed or roughly dressed masonry, sufficient indications remain to prove that this building is a Post-Gupta structure. The most noticeable feature in the Mundeśvarī temple is its plan; it is neither square nor circular, but hexagonal. Temples with such plans are extremely rare in India. The decorations consists of a broad round moulding at the base of the plinth of the same type as that at Bhumra and the stone-work of the earliest main shrine at Sarnath, near Benares. The plinth is further decorated with *Kīrttimukhas*, with garlands hanging as loops from their mouths, and tassels at the junctions of the loops. The carvings of the great stone door-frame consists of bands of arabesque work, superimposed panels containing single or double human figures, and other well recognised Gupta decorative *motifs*. The carvings of the pillars and pilasters of the windows, bearing neat *Chaitya*-windows on them, all proclaim the Mundeśvarī temple to be a direct descendant of Gupta temples proper, yet not very far removed from the age of the Early Guptas. As at Nachna Kuthara and Bhumra, as well as Aihole and Pattadkal, pierced stone-frames admit light into the interior and even the bottoms of the jambs of such window-frames bear the figures of the river goddesses, Gaṅgā and Yamunā. Fragments of bas-reliefs discovered by Mr. J. C. French, I.C.S., exhibit the general decadence of Post-Gupta plastic art.

Gupta architects evolved a temple-type in which there was provision for a covered path of circumambulation surrounding the sanctum, which was closed on three sides and which provided one entrance only and an open porch in front. The subsequent modifications of this temple type are beyond the limit of our discussion but in the Post-Gupta period we find the addition of a modest *Śikhara* without any other important changes. Excavations at Mundeśvarī and Śankargadh may yet reveal traces of a covered path of circumambulation.

CHAPTER V.

PLASTIC ART.

The general impression that the Gupta age is the Golden age of Indian culture is almost entirely dependent on the evidence of its plastic art. The plastic art of the Gupta period proper has been studied to some extent in one part and very much neglected in others. The prevalent idea of the denotation and connotation of the term is also vague and art-critics generally try to convey the idea of excellence by the use of the term "Gupta". Thus, the term "Gupta Art" has been applied to the early Cālukyan art of South-western India[1], though the Guptas had no connection either historically or culturally with the country over which the early Cālukyas ruled. The scanty resemblance in artistic ideals is solely due to the imitation of the North, which is noticeable in the 6th and the 7th centuries in all parts of the South, both in architecture and in art.

Gupta art is really a *renaissance* due to the transformation in the ideals of the people of Northern India in the 4th and 5th centuries A.D. This transformation was based, on an assimilation of what was old, an elimination of what was exotic and foreign and finally a synthetic production of

---

1 Coomaraswamy.—*A History of Indian and Indonesian Art pp. 75–6.*

something entirely new, which was essentially Indian. In order to determine the exact nature of this transformation it will be necessary in the first place to consider the antecedents of Gupta art and in the second place to analyse it into its different constituent elements; *i.e.*, to consider what Gupta art actually produced within the limits of the realms of the early Gupta empire. In other words, for a synthetic study of this great *renaissance*, it will be necessary to divide it according to its centres of activity or production. The greatest centres of artistic activity in the Gupta empire were the ancient Scythian capital of Mathurā, the great Buddhist stronghold of Benares, and finally the ancient metropolis of India, the venerable city of Pāṭaliputra. There were minor centres of activity, such as Eran or Airakiṇa, Daśapura, or Mandasor, etc. While the development of plastic art in the Buddhist city of Benares has been closely watched by the excavators during the last quarter of this century, the interest evinced by scholars in the history of the development of the history of the Mathurā school of art of this period has been more or less of a dillettante nature. That a school of art existed during the period of rule of the early Guptas in Northern India is not yet fully believed either by the scholar or by the artist. The stray sculptures of Udaigiri or Bhilsa, or Mandasor may have excited passing interest but the entire production of different centres has never been analysed on the same basis and, so far as I am aware, no attempt has been made for a general synthesis. To trace the graphical outline of the artistic development of the provinces of Northern India, it will be necessary to fall back on dated sculptures. There are a few produced by the Mathurā school, while the dates of the majority produced by the Benares school can be accurately deduced from the characters of their votive inscriptions and it is only in the metropolitan school that we are, even now, at a loss both for an adequate number of specimens and some data for deducing their dates.

In the Mathurā school, the traditions of the Kuṣāṇa school continued up to the middle of the 5th century A.D. Up to 448–9 the great quarries of mottled red sandstone at Karri produced material which was fashioned by artists of the Mathurā school and carried away to distant places. The image of Buddha, discovered at Mankuwar, in the Karchana *Tahsil* of the Allahabad district, dedicated in G.E. 129, during the reign of the emperor Kumāragupta I, is one of the latest examples of the migration of products of the Mathura school. Because the inscription states that the image is one of Buddha, therefore, it is possible for us to recognise it as a Buddhist image. The head is shaven and the posture is *abhaya*, very often adopted by Jinas also. The presence of the lions and the wheel on the pedestal do not help us. In its proportions, the treatment of the torso and the expression on the face of the main figure, this image, of 448-9

A.D., does not differ in the least from early Kuṣāṇa Buddhist images of the 1st and the 2nd century A.D. The Mankuwar image, therefore, serves as a typical example of a great conservative force in the Mathurā School of sculpture even in the middle of the 5th century A.D. Codrington is distinctly wrong in stating that "this figure, the standing Buddha in the Mathurā Museum, and the Sarnath Buddha, are the most perfect examples of Gupta sculpture. This (the Mankuwar image) is probably the earliest of the three, the Sarnath Buddha being the latest[1]". Among dated specimens of the Mathurā school, belonging to the Gupta period, there is another which is sixteen years earlier in date than the Mankuwar image. This is the Mathurā Jaina image of G.E. 113 dedicated during the reign of Kumāragupta I.[2] The generic resemblance between these two specimens is so very striking that it is difficult to determine for what reasons Codrington classifies the Mankuwar image with regular Gupta figures from Mathurā and Sarnath. With the exception of a very slight *Uṣṇīṣa* there is no indication in the Mankuwar image about its late date. The existence of a Jaina image from Mathurā of A.D. 432 was perhaps unknown to Messrs. Rothenstein and Codrington. This Jaina image is headless. The

---

1 Codrington and Rothenstein—*Ancient India*, p. 60.

2 *Epigraphia Indica*, Vol. II, p. 210, No. XXXIX.

modelling of the torso is typically early Kuṣāṇa in both images. The legs are shapeless and out of proportion in the Jaina image but the method in modelling is the same in this figure and the Mankuwar figure, which is absolutely different in the Sarnath seated Buddha (B (*b*) 181 of the Sarnath Museum.) The lions of the throne, the wheel, and its base and even the modelling of the Buddhas on the Mankuwar image and the kneeling worshippers on the Jaina specimen are typically Kuṣāṇa and do not show the regularity of proportion and equipoise of the regular Gupta type of images of the Benares school. These two images prove that there is marked differentia between the products of the Mathurā school and those of the Benares and Paṭaliputra School of the Gupta period; the marked features of the Kuṣāṇa School lingered on right up to the middle of the 5th century A.D., when they were modified by certain influences which were simultaneously at work all over the country.

Codrington states "The Gupta century provides a definite series of motives, which increases in number and imaginative complexity as the period of the great cave-temples draws near. It was at Ajanta, Aurangabad, and Elura that the mediæval period began. It stands for a definite culture, but one differing considerably from the Gupta. The one is classical, the other, romantic. Sir John Marshall is rightly stirred by the simplicity of the Gupta shrines. The 'refinement' and 'clear definition', not only of these little buildings, but of the sculpture that adorns them, is striking and unique"[1]. The time has now come for a broader and more definite delineation of the most marked features of Gupta art and it cannot be better illustrated than in the process of the metamorphosition of the Mathurā school of sculpture. The new ideal as expressed by the images of the beginning of the 5th century shows a close approximation to the style of Benares in its most noticeable features, *viz* :—

(1) The marked Mongoloid features of the upper part of the face, especially the long tangential eye-brows,

(2) The conventional arrangement of the draperies especially the disappearance of the lines indicating folds of garments and

(3) The enlargement of the halo to form a miniature back-slab and the introduction of the Gupta style in arabesques along its margin.

The introduction of this style in Benares itself is difficult to trace. Pandit (now Rai Bahadur) D. R. Sahni, the compiler of the catalogue of the Sarnath Museum of Archaeology, has not attempted it. A special study of the contents of the Sarnath Museum does not help in the least as all inscribed specimens show this particular feature, the first

---

[1] *Ancient India, p. 62.*

one mentioned above. In the Mathurā school the change is noticed in the first place by the final adoption of the curling hair and the *uṣṇīṣa* along with that of ornamental foliage and arabesques for the ornamentation of the halo. The most noticeable example is M.5 in the Indian Museum, Calcutta, in which the Mongoloid type of the eyes is to be noticed, perhaps, for the first time.[1] In the Mathurā school, the conventional lines indicating the folds of the drapery continued to be used for sometime and Buddha images of the Gupta period minus the lines of the drapery are rare. The best examples are A.5 in the Mathurā Museum.[2] During the rule of the early Guptas over Northern India the output of the Mathurā school of sculpture diminished steadily. Very few Jaina images were dedicated and most of the products, especially images, are either Hindu or Buddhistic. It cannot be said that Buddhism was yet on the decline, we have the testimony of Fa-Hsien on that point. It was flourishing exceedingly at Benares, though languishing at the Buddhist Holy of Holies, Mahābodhi, as proved both by the statement of Fa-Hsien and the paucity of images at that place. The reason of the general decline of the Mathurā school of sculpture must be, therefore, a decline in the material prosperity of the people of that city. Jainism, too, must

---

1 Anderson—*Catalogue and Handbook on the Archæological collection in the Indian Museum, Calcutta, part I, p. 181.*

2 Vogel—*Catalogue of the Mathurā Museum of Archæology, pp. 49–50, pl. IX.*

have declined, on the evidence of images, but it revived after Maḥmūd's sack of that city in 1018 A.D. The extent of the influence exerted by the Benares school over the older school of Mathurā can be better gauged by a comparison of two Buddha images of these two schools now in the Indian Museum, Calcutta, S.14 [1] and M.5. In these two the Mongoloid appearance of the upper part of the face and the tangential eyebrows are almost identical, the robes differ in the conventional lines indicating the drapery and there is more ornament on the halo of M.5 than in the case of S.14. This comparison will be sufficient to prove that the Mathurā school, at a later date in the Gupta period succumbed to the influences of the Benares School.

That there was a very ancient school of sculpture at Benares, at least, from the Post-Maurya period onwards, has been sufficiently demonstrated by the discoveries of Marshall and his assistants. In its heyday of glory the great Mathurā school of the Kuṣāṇa period succeeded in imposing its sway at Benares and images were brought from Mathurā for dedication at Benares and were also made locally in the Benares style. A certain number of images in the Sarnath Museum, in the Kuṣāṇa-Mathurā style show the use of red paint, which the sun-light and rain of eighteen centuries have partly effaced. Mr. Sahni has not expressed

---

[1] Anderson—*Catalogue and Handbook, etc., part II, pp. 11–12.*

any definite opinion on the origin of these painted images, but while the technique is Kuṣāṇa-Mathurā, the material is distinctly Chunar instead of Karri sandstone. In the third and fourth centuries A.D., there is a decline in the output, however meagre, and images of the post-Kuṣāṇa period are surprisingly few. Suddenly in the 5th century there is a great increase in plastic activity at Benares and a total change in the ideals of the artists. The new type of images betray very little connection with the old Kuṣāṇa type, but fortunately the number of inscribed specimens is so very great that it is possible to work out the dates of the gradual evolution both of images as well as of bas-reliefs. The earliest images discovered at Sarnath, which belong definitely to the Gupta period, are those which show the use of that particular form of *Ma* in which the base line is quite separate, being in fact a horizontal projection from the lower end of the right vertical. The earliest examples of this type of inscriptions were discovered by the excavators of Sarnath in the earlier part of the 19th century, the best examples of which is stele S.3.[1] This type of *Ma* is used throughout in the Karamdanda inscription of G. E. 117 of the reign of Kumāragupta I, but is not to be found in the Allahabad pillar inscription of Samudragupta or the two Mathurā inscriptions of Chandragupta II. In certain cases only, there

[1] *Ibid.*, p. 7.

is a modification of the features but these are exceptions to the general rule. The best examples are S.34[1] of the Indian Museum, Calcutta and the great *Dharma-cakra-Buddha-bhaṭṭāraka* discovered by Mr. F. O. Oertel in 1904–5.[2]

We have now to discuss the effects of the new Buddha-type in the eastern provinces of Northern India. The influence of the Benares school was more widely felt towards the east than to the west. The only reason for this appears to be the activity of the artists in the metropolitan district of the Gupta empire. Quarter of a century ago Gupta sculptures were exceedingly rare in Bihar and Bengal; but the recent excavations of Nālandā have thrown such a brilliant flood of light on the plastic art of the eastern countries of Northern India that it is no longer possible to deny the existence of such a school in and around Pāṭaliputra. The differentiative features of this eastern school we shall discuss later on. In connection with the Benares school we shall have to discuss its influence on that of Pāṭaliputra. Images discovered at Nālandā, both in stone and in metal, definitely prove that the first distinctive feature of the Benares school had permeated as far as Nālandā. This is noticeable both in early Gupta and later Gupta sculptures. The great metal image of Buddha discovered at Nālanda[3] shows the

---

[1] *Ibid.*, p. 19.

[2] *Catalogue of the Sarnath Museum of Archæology*, pp. 70-71, No. B(b) 181.

[3] *A History of Fine Art in India and Indonesia*, pl. XLII, fig. 161

tangential eyebrows, the schematic arrangement of the curls of hair and the typical *uṣṇīṣa* of the Benares school. It differs from the regular Benares type of Buddha in its stylistic arrangement of both the upper and the lower garments and in the presence of the conventional lines indicating the folds of the drapery. Exactly similar characteristics are to be observed in the large copper image of Buddha discovered at Sultanganj, in the Bhagalpur district, and now preserved in the Birmingham Museum.[1] In Buddha images these two characteristics differentiate the Pāṭaliputra school from that of Benares, which were handed down by post-Gupta artists to the great Eastern Indian School of mediæval sculpture (800-1200 A.D.). The curly fringe of the upper and lower garments along with the conventional lines indicating the folds of the drapery show the indebtedness of the Pāṭaliputra school to the Indo-Greek school of Gandhāra. For some time, the Mathurā school of the early Gupta period retained the lines of the drapery but the curly fringe disappeared early in the Kuṣāṇa period. The influence of the Benares school was exerted more strongly outside the metropolitan province of the Gupta empire. An image of Buddha discovered at Biharoil, in the Rajshahi district of Bengal, is distinctly of the Benares type, so much so that it deluded Rai Bahadur Pandit Dayaram Sahni, M.A., into believing that it was actually made

---

1 *Ibid., pl. XLI, fig. 160.*

at Benares and transported to Northern Bengal for dedication. The technique is distinctly that of the Benares school in its entirety, but the material is not Chunar sandstone, thereby proving that mere identity of features and technique do not indicate locality so far as the Benares school is concerned. The Biharoil image shows the curly fringe of the drapery gathered together in the proper left hand. Moreover, the tangential eye-brows are less pronounced. The eastward extension of the influence of the Benares school was further demonstrated by the discoveries at Dah Parbatiya, near Tezpur in Assam, of a stone door, frame of the Gupta period in which the moulding of the forms of the river goddesses, Ganges and Yamunā, at the bottom of the jambs is distinctly reminiscent of the Benares school [1] and at the same time different from the mouldings of similar forms on the jamb from Besnagar now in the Boston Museum of Fine Art.[2]

In figure-work the influence of the Benares school is less distinct in Central India. It is present to some extent only in the *Eka-mukha-liṅgas* discovered by the writer at Khoh and Bhumra, in the Nagod State of Central India. In the case of the face on the *liṅga* at Khoh, the eye-brows

---

1 *Ibid., 1924–25, pp. 98-9. pl. XXXII a-c.*

2 Coomaraswamy—*A History of Fine Art in India and Indonesia. pl. XLVII, fig. 177.*

are only slightly elevated.[1] But in that at Bhumra the tangential stroke is more pronounced.[2] They are altogether wanting in the rather primitive figure of Viṣṇu in cave No. II at Udaygiri, near Bhilsa in the dominions of the Mahārājā Scindia.

Further on it is impossible to trace the influence of the new type of the human figure as evolved by the artists of the Benares school of sculpture of the early Gupta period. In one respect, the three great schools of Gupta sculpture agree, which is their method of treatment of bas-reliefs. Another important feature of all Gupta schools is the introduction of subjects from the orthodox Brahmanical or Hindu religion into bas-reliefs and on this subject all the three great northern schools as well as their offshoots agree. Bas-reliefs, primarily employed for the depiction of the *Buddha-Carita* or the *Jātakas* began to be employed for the depiction of scenes of Hindu mythology the best known examples of which are the great lintels from Gadhwa in the Allahabad district, now in the Lucknow museum, and the three great panels on the Daśāvatāra temple at Deogadh, in the Jhansi district. It is in the separate treatment of these bas-reliefs discovered at Rajaona, in the Munger[3]

---

[1] *Progress Report of the Archæological Survey of India, Western Circle, for the year ending 31st March 1920, pl. XXIX.*

[2] *Memoirs of the Archæological Survey of India No. 16 ; The temple of Siva at Bhumara, pl. XV (c).*

[3] These pillars with the bas-reliefs were wrongly described by me

district and those at Nālandā that the distinct features of the Pāṭaliputra school came to be recognised.

The Pāṭaliputra school of sculpture still remains to be studied as a distinct and separate movement in the plastic activity of the Gupta period. The remains, except at Nālandā, are few and yet inconsiderable so far as images are concerned. But we are more fortunate in the case of bas-reliefs. Certain images from Nālandā have been referred to the Gupta period by the successive excavators of that site but, it appears to me, without sufficient reason. In the Eastern provinces it is rather difficult to distinguish between early Gupta and Post-Gupta sculptures. Consequently unless we proceed on the basis of inscribed specimens it will be difficult to arrive at any satisfactory conclusion. Inscribed images of the Early Gupta period are still very few in North-eastern India and those that have been discovered at Nālandā or Mahābodhi show certain characteristics which are different from those of the Benares school. All such images are Buddhist and the difference lies in the modelling. The Benares school shows the return of the human figure to the normal in all images except those of the Buddha in which abnormalities remain in the shape of unna-

---

as coming from Chandimau in the Patna District in *Ann. Rep. Arch. Survey of India*, 1911-12. They were originally discovered at Rajaona in the Munger District *Vide* Cunningham.—*Arch Survey Reports, Vol, III, pp. 154-5.*

turally long ears, the tangential eye-brows, etc., but we do not find any of these signs in Bodhisatva figures. The order of the Bodhisatvas, according to celestial adherence or Dhyānī Buddhas, is introduced for the first time with prominence in the Benares school. This is to be seen in images of Lokeśvara which bear a comparatively large figure of Amitābha on the head. It took sometime to reconcile the artist to the idea of celestial adherence in Benares and to make the Dhyānī Buddha a miniature figure, more decorative than expressive, on the crown or the head-dress of the Bodhisatva. In the Pāṭaliputra school we find that, even in the middle of the 5th century A.D., the idea of celestial adherence had been quietly assimilated by the artists of the metropolitan school and unnaturally large figures are altogether absent.

In the treatment of the human figure, Gupta artists all over India, are characterised by their uncommon devotion to real naturalism and symmetry and total rejection of all mannerisms introduced into the Mathurā school of the Kuṣāṇa period. Such mannerisms are noticeable in very early and late Mathurā-Kusāṇa products and a certain class of them are totally devoid of all sorts of artistic convention. Such are the splendid torsos and heads recovered by Führer from different mounds of Mathurā towards the close of the last century.[1]

1 Now in the Lucknow Museum.

It is in this characteristic that the strongest appeal of Gupta art really lies. Codrington says, "Gupta art has been praised for its intellectuality. It would be better to treat it as the natural outcome of ancient Indian art, with its vivid appreciation of form and pattern, and its love of the quick beat and rhythm of living things and of their poise and balance in repose."[1] The poise and balance or in other words, real naturalism, and symmetry were introduced into Gupta art after some effort. The sculptures in the Udaigiri caves, near Bhilsa in the Gwalior State, for example, do not all belong to one and the same date, and consequently, they betray different stages in the progress of local art. The images in the verandah of the Sanakānīka cave at Udaigiri all betray a certain amount of stilted and stiff expression which we do not find in the next reign, *i.e.*, that of Kumāragupta I. The development of the door-frame is also incomplete and the carved door-frame in this cave[2] compares very unfavourably with those of the temples at Bhumra[3] and Nachna Kuthara[4], and Deogadh. The same characteristics are to be observed in the Śeṣa-śāyin in another cave as well as the smaller sculptures in Vīrasena's Cave or Cave No. 6 at

---

1 Rothenstein—*Ancient India, p. 62.* 2 *Ibid., pl. 29A.*

3 *Memoirs of the Archæological Survey of India; the temple of Śiva at Bhumra, pl. III.*

4 *Progress Report of the Archæological Survey of India, Western Circle, for the year ending 31st March 1919, pl. XVI.*

the same place. Even the elaborate door-frame or Candragupta's cave at the same place is not of this type.[1] A change is to be noticed in the Varāha or the great Boar incarnation which is very close to Vīrasena's cave, in which the elasticity of all the figures, including the quardruple frieze of gods on the adjoining wall shows that the new impulse was already working. Vīrasena's cave and the Sanakānīka cave belong very definitely to the reign of Candragupta II and from these three specimens of plastic art it appears certain that the zenith of excellence was reached by Gupta artist during the reign of Kumāragupta I. The same conclusion is also apparent from the execution of dies. The finest coin issued by a Gupta mint-master is undoubtedly the Peacock type of Kumāragupta I. Another point noticeable in the Varāha cave is the grace and elasticity of the figure of Pṛthvī, a slight figure, poised lightly on the left shoulder of the Boar, and grasping the dreadful snout caressingly. The same amount of poise and elasticity is also to be observed in the figure of the Nāga and the headless figure behind it.[2]

To another portion of Central India belongs the credit of possessing the best examples of facial expression in Gupta art. I do not think that the face on the *Eka-mukha-liṅga* at Khoh has been surpassed in this direction. That on the specimen

---

[1] *Ancient India, pl. 33 B. & C.*

[2] William Cohn—*Indische plastik, Tafels 22–23.*

found inside the temple at Bhumra also belongs to the foremost rank, but the figure of the kneeling dwarf discovered by the writer at Khoh certainly stands second only to the *liṅga* at Khoh[1]. The face of the Gaṇeśa discovered inside one of the smaller temples in front of the bigger temple of Śiva at Bhumra is also natural but inexpressive.[2] Much more expressive is the bust of Śiva [3] on the boss of the lintel at Bhumra compared to which the face of Nārāyaṇa on the boss of the lintel of the Daśāvatara temple at Deodgadh is mute.

We must now pass on to the next great division of Gupta plastic art, bas-reliefs. Going back to the Benares school we find a new class of Buddhist stelae, in which the decorative influence of Gāndhāran art is clearly manifest. Such stelae are met with for the first time in India proper and are used solely to depict the principal scenes of Buddha's life. They fall into two classes: (*a*) stelae with eight principal or more scenes from the Buddha's life and (*b*) those portraying a single incident of the Buddha's life, *e.g.*, the great miracle of Śrāvastī. In the first class, the arrangement of single or double superimposed panels clearly indicate that the scheme was borrowed from the style of side-decoration of niches in Gāndhāran *Stūpas*, in which there were single or double

1 *Progress Report of the Archæological Survey of India, Western Circle, for the year ending 31st March, 1920, pl. XXX.*

2 *Memoirs of the Archæological Survey, No. 16, pl. XV (a).*

3 *Ibid., pl. III (b).*

oblong superimposed panels on the sides and curved panels, enclosed within one or more arches, at the top. This scheme does not generally appear in the Mathurā school though superimposed panels containing bas-reliefs are to be found on the backs of pillars.[1] Scenes from Buddha's life in the Mathurā school have been found for the greater part on architraves, either in single or double rows, separately. Such stelae of the Benares school are, therefore, an innovation peculiar to that locality, many examples of which were discovered in the previous century. Examples of such stelae are to be found in the museums at Calcutta and Sarnath only. Stelae with the principal incidents of Buddha's life can, again, be divided into two classes:—(i) More elaborate and (ii) less elaborate. In the first class are to be placed such stelae which contain more than four scenes of the Master's life and usually eight. Such are S.1 of the Indian Museum, Calcutta and C (a) 3 of the Sarnath Museum. These stelae are usually divided into several horizontal rows, each containing at least two panels with bas-reliefs. In the second class are to be placed such bas-reliefs in which there is only one series of four superimposed panels usually containing the four principal incidents of Buddha's life; such as S.3 of the Calcutta Museum and C (a) 1 of the Sarnath Museum.[2]

---

1 Anderson—*Catalogue and Handbook, part I., pp. 186–90.*

2 Vogel and Sahni—*Catalogue of the Museum of Archæology at Sarnath, pl. XIX.*

The Calcutta Museum possesses a peculiar stele which bears three superimposed bas-reliefs. This stele must have stood separate yet it does not begin with the birth or Māyā's dream about her conception and does not end with the *Mahāparinirvāṇa.* This peculiar stelae contains the scene of Perfect Enlightenment at the bottom combined with the allurement of Māra's daughters and the attack of Māra's army, the first sermon in the centre, and the *Devāvatāra* near the top. It is difficult to judge whether there were bas-reliefs over the top (S. 4).[1] Stele bearing single incidents of Buddha's life become more important in the Benares school and the most prominent incident chosen was the great miracle of Śrāvastī, S. 5 in the Indian Museum, Calcutta and C (a) 6 of the Sarnath Museum.[2] Other incidents are also, common but rarely represented; such as Buddha at the time of the Perfect Enlightenment dedicated by the Buddhist elder (*Sthavira*) Bandhugupta.[3] These stelae were the peculiar creations of the artists of the Benares school and they do not seem to have found favour anywhere outside the limits of Buddhist Benares. Very few specimens of this particular type of stelae have been discovered elsewhere. Subsequent schools adopted and elaborated the ideas of the Benares school and some adopted the system of separate images, but

---

1 Anderson—*Catalague and Handbook, part II, p. 7.*

2 *Catalague of the Museum of the Archæology at Sarnath, pl. XXI.*

3 *Ibid., pl. IX.*

none used the superimposed stele of the Benares type.

In other respects the Gupta school at Benares is rather poor in bas-reliefs. The only superior example is the great lintel with the Kshāntivādin *Jātaka*, in which there are altogether six panels.[1] Even in this specimen, the Benares school suffers in our estimation compared with the Pātaliputra school. There is a certain lack of dignity in the figures of this bas-relief which is divided into six parts by being enclosed by six conventional *Caitya*-windows. The first and the last panels contain figures of Jambhala, of which one is a very crude bit of carving.[2] The second panel from the proper left shows a better idea of proportion in the case of the Bodhisatva but a neglect of it in the case of the dancing girls.[3] The third panel, that of the dance is on the whole better balanced and would compare favourable with other bas-reliefs.[4] But the artist lost his head when he came to panel 5 and there is a total want of poise and balance in the figure of the king which is not the case anywhere else in the Gupta bas-reliefs. The figure of the king or the executioner appears to be toppling over the head of the ascetic Bodhisatva.[5] If we compare this bas-relief with those on the pillars from Rajaona, we find that the Benares school is far behind the general standard of excel-

---

1 *Ibid., pp. 233-4, pl. XXIII.*
2 *Ibid., pl. XXIV.*
3 *Ibid., pl. XXV.*
4 *Ibid., pls. XXVI-XXVII.*
5 *Ibid., pl. XXVIII.*

ence than the Pātaliputra school of the same period. The penance of Arjuna surrounded by four pits of fire and the separation of this scene from his departure to Indra's heaven with Mātuli is far superior in vivacity, arrangement, and to some extent even in perspective to all bas-reliefs of the Benares school. In the second panel from Rajaona, which is better preserved, the different events narrated in proper sequence of the fight between Śiva and Arjuna and Siva's blessing are not separated by any ornaments but show superior poise and virility. Even the giant horned-*Kīrtti-mukhas* are far superior to any discovered in Benares or anywhere else.

It is in the treatment of the bas-reliefs that we notice for the first time another difference between the Gupta schools of the East and the Centre; the treatment of the female bust. Female figures of the Mathurā school, which can be definitely assigned to the Gupta period are very rare, but such figures are more abundant in Central India and in the Eastern countries. A comparison instituted between the busts of female figures discovered at Besnagar,[1] Pathari,[2] Benares,[3] Rajgir,[4] and Tezpur[5] in Assam prove that the artists of North-

---

1 Coomaraswamy—*History of Fine Art in India and Indonesia, fig.* 177.

2 *Ibid., fig.* 178.

3 *Catalogue of the Sarnath Museum of Archæology, pl.* XXVI-XXVII.

4 *History of Fine Art in India and Indonesia, fig.* 176.

5 *Annual Report of the Archæological Survey of India, 1924-25, pl.* XXXII a-c.

western and West-central India depicted full over-developed busts of the aboriginal type, while those of the East followed the more slender development of the female torso in the North-eastern Provinces. The difference is perhaps much more accentuated in the bust of the *Apsarās*, an accessory figure in one of the images in the Gwalior museum.[1]

A tendency is growing in recent years to call all contiguous phases of *renaissance* in art in distant provinces of India, "Gupta." Such mistaken terminology are being used by well-known art critics like Coomaraswamy. Coomaraswamy says "There exists many 'caves' of the Gupta period. At Ajanta caves, XVI and XVII are *Vihāras* dating about 500 A.D., Cave XIX a *caitya*-hall datable about 550; all of these contain paintings, referred to below.[2]" Similarly with regard to the Viśvakarmā *caitya*-hall the same author says "the excavation is Gupta or early Cālukya dating about 600.[3]" There is no contiguity either in date or in locality between early Gupta art and those of Ajanta, Ellora, or Badami. It is extremely doubtful whether any paintings in any of the caves at Ajanta can be referred to the fifth century A.D., the earlier paintings belong to the pre-Christian centuries and those in the later caves bearing painted labels are certainly not earlier than 600 A.D. Neither Ajanta nor Ellora nor Badami

---

1 *History of Fine Art in India and Indonesia, fig. 173.*

2 *Ibid.*, p. 76. *Ibid.*, p. 77.

were ever included within the dominions of the Gupta emperors and their artists did not begin work before the final destruction of the Gupta empire. Such authors often date specimens without stating any reasons, reliable or unreliable, and the absence of data never deters them from coining incongruous terms and nomenclature. The only authorities which Coomaraswamy can quote about the date of the Viśvakaramā *caitya*-hall are Fergusson and Burgess, none of whom were ever competent to date an Indian monument from an inscription. It is *prima facie* wrong to give a proper name to a movement, when it takes place at a different locality, and at a much later date. Coomaraswamy and others want to express the idea that the symmetry and poise, introduced into northern art some time in the 5th century A.D., appears in the art of south-western India also a century and a half later. It was a *renaissance* in art, the impulse having been felt much earlier in the north than in the south-west; but for that reason it is not necessary to design it in a way which is distinctly misleading.

The time when the early Gupta empire was crumbling to pieces and when the Hūṇas had already advanced into the centre of India, saw the rise of a remarkable group of monuments in Central India, all of which denote a step in Gupta plastic art. Eran is already known to us as the findspot of a number of important inscriptions, the most important of which were inscribed towards the close of the 5th, and the beginning of the 6th century A.D. One of the latest of these records are incised on a pillar which is the *dhvaja-stambha* of Viṣṇu erected by the brothers, Mātṛ-viṣṇu and Dhanya-viṣṇu, when Suraśmicandra was the Viceroy of the country between the Yamunā and Narmadā. This pillar can be easily recognised by the presence of a figure of Garuḍa on its top bearing on it the wheel of Viṣṇu. It lies at a distance from the temple of the Boar and was erected in G.E., 165=484-5 A.D. Close to it is the second pillar which bears on it a record of Goparāja, the general of Bhānugupta who died here in a battle with the Hūṇas in 191=510-1 A.D. All over the highlands, on which these two pillars are situated, can be seen ruins and images. The most important of them is the colossal figure of the Boar incarnation of Viṣṇu which was dedicated by Dhanya-viṣṇu, after the death of his brother Mātṛ-viṣṇu, in the first year of the reign of Toramāṇa, the Hūṇa king. This Boar is slightly different in conception from that in the cave of Udaygiri near Bhilsa as it portrays a quadruped mammal and not a human figure with a Boar's head. As an object of art this colossal figure is an abject failure. It resembles an elephant more than a boar and anatomical details have been grossly neglected. So much so, that it cannot bear any comparison with the Udaygiri boar. By the side of this boar stands a beautiful porch of a temple on four-fluted columns, of the Bhumra type, bearing cruciform capitals with winged figures below them. This is only a part of the early Gupta temple enshrining a big image of Viṣṇu, still *in situ.* In style, this figure is far superior to that of the Earth goddess depicted on the breast of the boar and it seems that the temple of Viṣṇu and the image of the god are both earlier than the Boar. This image of Viṣṇu, the only specimen known to us belonging to the early Gupta period, shows a definite decline in the portrayal of the human figure, when compared to the little image of Gaṇeśa and the two attendant figures discovered at Bhumra in 1920.

Only one class of images remains to be discussed, about which very little is known; metal-casting. The discovery of the metal image of Buddha at Nālandā was preceded by that of a colossal figure of Buddha at Sultanganj in the Bhagalpur district in the last century. With the exception of these two figures very few metal specimens of the early Gupta period are known to us. Stray images in metal have been discovered at different places and many writers commit the mistake of herding them together. Thus, Coomaraswamy says that among Gupta sculpture in metal should be included the Sultanganj image and "other important examples include the richly decorated, copper and silver inlaid, brass figure (fig. 163) from Fatehpur, Kangra; the Boston bronze Buddha, said to have been found in Burma (fig. 159); and the rather clumsy statuettes from the Banda district, Bengal; and the fragments from Bezwada; small gold Buddha in the British Museum"[1].

If anything produced in India which is graceful can be called Gupta then only all these specimens can be relegated to the Gupta period. The Banda statuettes belong more to Central India than to Bengal as the Banda district is in the southern part of the United Provinces and they belong to Chandella rather than Gupta art as they were produced in the 11th century A.D. The Buddha figure from Kangra may be Post-Gupta but the figure in the Boston Museum has no connection with the Early or Post-Gupta period. The fragments from Bezwada certainly belong to the 10th century A.D; while the figure in the British Museum is scarcely earlier. The Sultanganj image provides a second specimen of the Pataliputra school, in which, like the Gupta school at Mathurā, the lines of the drapery were not eradicated. The face is also of a different type and a comparison with that of the metal figure in the Boston Museum shows clearly that the latter is centuries late in date.

The very high reputation which Gupta Schools of Art enjoy, at the present day, depends much more on architectural and artistic decorative *motifs* employed by them. One of the most

---

[1] *History of Fine Art in India and Indonesia p. 85.*

important evolutions in decorative *motifs* is the stylization of the *caitya*-window, a subject which has not received the amount of attention which it deserves. The high pointed opening in the upper part of the facades of *caitya-gharas* or Buddhist cathedral-halls lost their grandeur early in the Gupta period. A comparison of the facade of the *caitya*-halls at Karla and Bhaja, in the Poona district with those at Nasik and Kanheri will prove that the great horse-shoe-shaped window was fast diminishing in size.[1] From the middle second century B.C., the shape of the *caitya*-window became a favourite design for the decoration of the solid walls of the *Caitya*-halls and door-lintels.[2] The increase in the side wings of the design is apparent in the Gupta period. In actual *Caitya*-halls we find it late in the 6th century in the facade of Cave No.19 at Ajanta.[3] As an architectural *motif* the increase in the size of the side wings made it possible to use it in diverse ways. Another innovation was the conversion of the *Caitya*-window into a regular tre-foil arch as in the facade of the later Viśvakarmā-at Ellora.[4] But the evolution of the stylized *Caitya*-windows from the 6th to the 12th century A.D., is beyond the scope of this enquiry.

In the main shrine at Sarnath, numerous *caitya*-windows were used in the older structure of the

---

1 Codrington—*Ancient India, pls. 4–5.*

2 *Ibid., pl. 6.* 3 *Ibid., pl. 36A ; 37B.*

4 *History of Fine Art, in India and Indonesia fig. 155.*

Gupta period, when that monument was rebuilt with stone. Some of these stones, specially the carved ones, were again used in the construction of the plinth when that temple was rebuilt in brick in the 9th or 10th century A.D. At this time, certain *caitya*-windows were used for the construction of the lowest plinth line. The comparison of the *caitya*-windows in stone, both fragmentary and entire, in the plinth of the main shrine at Sarnath enables us to declare that that shrine, as it was discovered in 1904–05, cannot be a monument of the early Gupta Age. The Museum of Archæology at Sarnath now becomes very useful to the student of Gupta Art, as it contains the best collection of *caitya*-windows of the Gupta period. Unfortunately for us, the learned compiler of its Catalogue, Rai Bahadur Pandit Dayaram Sahni, M.A., now Deputy Director of Archæology in India for exploration, could not find suitable terminology for the expression of his ideas, and therefore, it is extremely difficult to find out which section of the catalogue contains his description of this famous collection of *caitya*-windows. All of them are described under the heading "D(i).–Pediments and face-stones."[1] Some of them are undoubtedly pediments as they are stones from plinth-mouldings and string-courses of early Gupta buildings; but it is very difficult to understand what is meant by face-stones. As has been

[1] *Catalogue of the Museum of Archæology at Sarnath*, pp. 254–64.

demonstrated above the *caitya*-window was used at Bhumra and Deogadh as a free-standing decorative *motif* and was used later on in relief against members of architecture. The large and small *caitya*-windows discovered at Bhumra were, no doubt, used along the cornice of the temple, alternately according to size, and as the majority of the Sarnath specimens belong to this variety, they should not have been styled "face-stones". As at Bhumra, the *caitya*-window of the Gupta period is really a trefoil in which the central arc is larger than the side ones and in which the side arcs are still leaf-shaped rather than arcs proper. In the middle of the larger arc is to be found a circular sunken panel, usually called the medallion. The rim or circumference of this medallion is enclosed by a line of beads, the place of which is sometimes taken by rosettes as at Deogadh. The rest of the interspaces, specially the space in the side wings is occupied with small lotus rosettes or arabesque.[1] The Sarnath Museum can boast of a much greater variety in the contents of these *caitya*-windows than any other site of early Gupta date. The best specimens show a seated or standing figure of some deity as in the Bhumra medallions and in certain cases only a running cupid.[2] In many cases the medallion is filled up with a large lion's head. At this stage, we are

---

1 *Memoirs of the Archæological Survey of India No. 16, the temple of Śiva at Bhumara. pl. XIII a-c.*

2 *Ibid., pl. III (a).*

introduced to a new style in *caitya*-windows, the best examples of which are to be found on the lintel bearing the representation of the Kshānti-vādin *Jataka.* In this case the *caitya*-window *motifs* are placed in relief in front of a miniature temple crowned by an *Āmalaka.* The *caitya*-window has changed its shape by the metamorphosition of the circular medallion into a trefoil medallion. The sides of the circle have separated and between these two semi-circles is introduced an ellipsoid curve at the top. The introduction of this new member causes the *caitya*-window itself to become divided into two unequal parts with two side-wings on each side instead of one. The Central arc of the *Caitya*-window contains the curved end of the ellipse and is supported at the end of the upper part on two square pilasters. Such trefoils contain standing figures of deities.[1] In the second class, we find that though the *caitya*-window proper has become divided into two parts, with two side-wings on each side, there is no connection between the upper half and the lower. In the upper half the medallion is almost a complete circle and contains, in the majority of cases, a horned lion with arabesque as its mane. Such *caitya*-windows are interposed along the beam of the lintel between the larger ones. The medallion, in the lower part,

---

1. *Catalogue of the Museum of Archæology at Sarnath, pl. XXIII, XXV.*

is shaped roughly like an ellipse and consists of two semi-circles joined together by parallel straight lines. They contain figures of dwarfs of the Bhumra and Deogadh types.[1] The contents of such medallions in the Sarnath collection of free-standing *Caitya*-windows is varied, the most important among which are the types which contain figures of animals, not to be found in other schools except that of Benares. In certain cases we find Buddha, in others, figures of minor deities as at Bhumra, but in the majority of cases we find Kīrttimukhas or lion's heads. In one particular case the *caitya*-window being placed in an angle of a plinth-moulding its medallion is obscured and can hardly be seen. Here, the ingenuity of the artist is displayed by the representation of a portion of the lion's face instead of the entire front. (D. i. 21.) In certain cases the front paws of the lion are also shown in addition. Many of the Sarnath medallions contain Buddhas in the *Bhūmisparśa mudrā*. In one case there is a four armed male holding a rosary, wheel, and a vase.[2] In certain cases, the medallion is a trefoil and contains the figure of a Buddha in the *Abhaya mudrā*. Many similar medallions contain a pair of pilasters with cruciform bracket capitals.[3] In other cases there is a row of dentils, just below

---

1 *Ibid.*, *pl. XXVIII*.

2 *Catalogue of the Museum of Archæology at Sarnath*, *pl.* 255, *No. D(i) 16.*

3 *Ibid.*, *p.* 257 *No. D(i) 29.*

the *Caitya*-windows, shaped as grotesque lion's heads.[1]

The peculiarly fashioned pillars or pilasters of the Gupta period are to be found in all three schools as well as in Central India. The earliest examples of such pillars or pilasters discovered during the Mathurā excavations of the previous century were brought to public notice by the late Dr. V.A. Smith.[2] The principal characteristic of such pillars and pilasters is that the lower half or third is generally square in section and quite plain. This plain portion ends in four single or double projections, one on each face, one set containing arabesques or some other ornaments, and the second half or three-quarters circular panels also containing ornaments. Above this portion the shaft is octogonal or hexagonal and round and bears on it one or more projections bearing either ornaments or arabesque. In the majority of cases such pillars or pilasters emerge from the wide mouth of a low vase with foliage at the corners. In many cases there is a round band ornamented with a twisted rope of pearls or other ornaments, which acts as a cushion for the abacus. In the case of the Mathurā pillars, the square projections, immediately above the plain portion, contains panels with grotesque animal figures emerging out of a mass of exquisite arabesque and the semi-

---

1 *Ibid., p. 258. No. D(i) 42.*

2 *Oxford History of India, 2nd edition, p. 160.*

circular panels above contain lotus rosettes. Between these panels and the cushion ornamented with the twisting-rope pattern there are two heavy projections, one bearing *gaṇas* alternated with *Kīrttimukhas* and another with horned-lion *Kīrttimukhas*. Many Sarnath specimens show the vase with foliage at the corners at the bottom while many others show the foliage and the vaṣe near the top.[1] The stilted style of expression of Rai Bahadur Dayaram Sahni, the compiler of the Sarnath catalogue, makes it extremely difficult to understand the details of the ornamentations on any of the sixty pillars which he has attempted to describe. A fine example, D(f)31 has been dismissed with a few words but a fuller description is certainly needed. One can feel the touch of the learned editor of this catalogue in footnotes where the affinities between the Mathurā and Sarnath style in Gupta pillars are discussed and pointed out.[2]

The best examples of the Pāṭaliputra school are the fragmentary pillars from Rajaona, in which the lower parts are perfectly plain and square but the centre bears two projections on each face. Each of the faces of the lower projection bears a panel enclosed within raised rims. These panels have a small pilaster on each side and contain bas-reliefs; Bhagīratha praying before Śiva on

[1] *Catalogue of the Museum of Archæology at Sarnath*, pp. 239–45.

[2] *Ibid.*, p. 239, Note 1 and p. 240, Note 2, quoting Smith's *Jain Stūpa*, pl. XLVI, Fig. 3.

Kailāsa, the Ganges coming to the earth on her *Vāhana*, a *Makara*, Arjuna receiving the boon from Śiva and then seeing Śiva and Pārvatī on Kailāsa, etc. Just above the projection there is a smaller projection, also oblong in shape, containing a regular semi-circular medallion and arabesque foliage in the triangular spaces left between the periphery of the circle and the sides of the pillar. The majority of the semi-circular medallions contain horned lions' heads or *Kīrttimukhas* but some bear winged figures or *Suparṇas*, whose lower parts end in magnificent spirals of arabesques.[1] The two or three pillars discovered during the recent excavations of the temple of Daśāvatāra at Deogadh perhaps score distinct merit as being larger than any others belonging to the Gupta period. In decoration they are exactly identical but much taller than the Rajaona, Bhumra or any of the Benares pillars. The style of art is perhaps slightly degenerate compared with that of Bhumra, but in point of execution of the bas-reliefs, those of the Pāṭaliputra school are undoubtedly the best.

Unfortunately specimens of architecture of the Pāṭaliputra school are so very meagre that it is not possible to speak much about its products. The excavations of Nālandā have yielded much that is important,[2] but was used in later periods

---

[1] *Annual Report of the Archæological Survey of India, 1911-12, pl. LXXIII-LXXV.*

[2] No connected and reliable account of the Nālandā finds have been published and the accounts published after the transfer of Dr. Hirananda Śāstrī, M.A., M.O.L., Ph.D., from the Central Circle of the

during the successive reconstructions under the Pālas of Bengal. The only specimen of the Pāṭaliputra school worth mentioning is the exquisite door-frame discovered by the writer at Dah Parbatiya near the town of Tezpur in the Darrang district of Assam. This door-frame though not connected with any dated inscription is undoubtedly Gupta because of its use of—

(1) trefoil medallions in *Caitya*-windows on the lintel,

(2) the use of the figures of river goddesses on the lower part of jambs,

(3) the false recessed angles of the lintel,

(4) the flying figure in high relief in the centre of the lower part of the lintel, and

(5) the particularly expressive figures of *gaṇas* on the arms of the cruciform bracket capitals of the pilasters.

This beautiful lintel is one of the best specimens of its class of the Gupta period. The carving on the jambs is continued overhead in four out of five bands. The lower part of the jambs consists of single panels, in very high relief against which are the figures of the river goddesses with female attendants on each side. The river goddesses exceed the limits of the panel but the attendant figurines have been kept very well within bounds. There are three attendants in the case of Gaṅgā

Archæological Survey of India, are too meagre and unscientific, being for the most part written by persons not qualified to undertake such tasks.

on the right, but two only in that of Yamunā to the left. Behind the back of each figure appear two flying geese pecking at the halo of the goddess, a new feature in the Gupta art. There are five bands of ornaments on each jamb :—

(1) a meandering creeper rising above the head of a Nāga,

(2) the body of the Nāga and the Nāgī rising from the top of the square panel at the bottom of each jamb and continued between the first and second bands on the lintel. The tails of these two serpents are held by the figure of Garuḍa in high relief aganist the lower part of the lintel, and

(3) ornamental foliage consisting of a straight stem with *amorini* clinging to it. These three bands are continued overhead on the lintel as its lowermost bands of ornaments.

(4) A pilaster, square in section bearing on it square bosses covered with arabesque as projections, which acts as supports to a number of human or divine figures and ends in a cruciform bracket capital.

(5) A double intertwined creeper forming conventional rosettes which is continued on the side projection of the lintel.

The lintel consists of a separate piece in which the lower part bears the first three bands of the jambs. The fourth band, the pilaster appears to support an architrave bearing on it five *caitya*-windows of two different types: (*a*) a trefoil in which all three arcs are of the same size; there are three *caitya*-windows with such medallions, one in the centre and two near the ends; (*b*) also trefoils in which the upper arc is larger than the two arcs on the sides. The central medallion of these five contains a seated figure of Śiva as Lākulīśa.

Compared with this elaborate door-frame the one at Bhumra is much simpler though the ornamentation is of a much higher standard of artistic excellence.[1] The door-frame of the early Gupta temple at Nachna Kuthara is exactly of the same type. Unfortunately a part of the lintel is missing and therefore we cannot judge whether there was a figure in high relief in the centre of the lower part of the lintel or not. Here also we find five bands, two of which only are continued over the lintel :—

(1) a meandering creeper,
(2) a super-imposed row of sunken panels containing human or divine figures,
(3) a geometrical pattern consisting of diamond shaped ornaments formed by the crossing of parallel lines,
(4) a pilaster, and

---

[1] *Memoirs of the Archæological Survey of India, No. 16; the temple of Śiva at Bhumara, pl. III(a).*

(5) a super-imposed row of half opened rosettes.

The first and the fifth bands are continued partly or wholly over the lintel. The second band turns into a row of flying figures as at Bhumra and the fifth band ends with the lintel, its continuation being a modified acanthus leaf pattern as at Bhumra.[1] At Nachna Kuthara the false projection of the lintel over the sides of the jambs contain two female figures with a single *gaṇa*[2] and not a pair as at Bhumra. The door-frame of the Daśāvatāra temple is exactly of a similar type. The points of resemblance are :—

(1) the presence of a divine figure in relief in the centre of the lower part of the lintel,

(2) the continuation of certain bands of ornaments of the jambs on the lintel,

(3) the false projection of the lintel over the sides of the jambs, and

(4) the presence of two pilasters supporting eaves or a roof as at Dah Parbatiya and Bhumra.

As the Daśāvatāra temple is later than the early Gupta temples at Bhumra and Nachna Kuthara, the ornamentation is more profuse ; but on account of the chastely bare side walls they

---

1 *Ibid., pl. VII(b).*

2 Codrington—*Ancient India, pl. 33, C.*

are very well balanced. The increase in the number of large human figures at the bottom of the jambs and a corresponding increase in the width of the jambs is compensated by a greater width of the lintel. As at Bhumra the topmost course of the lintel is a row of dentils shaped as *Kīrttimukhas*. Here there is a *caitya*-window at each end of the eaves and a modified one in the centre, which, however, is without a medallion. At Deogadh all three *caitya*-windows are complete. There is one at the unbroken end of the early Gupta temple at Nachna Kuthara while there are five on the door-frame at Dah Parbatiya. In the succeeding century, there was a change; in the Post-Gupta temple at Nachna Kuthara, there are three complete *caitya*-windows on the eaves supported by pilasters, but there is no divine figure in high relief in the centre of the lower part of the lintel. For this reason alone the door-frame at Dah Parbitya appears to be older than that of the Post-Gupta temple at Nachna Kuthara. The Deogadh temple shows a marked difference in the object of worship, which is a huge *liṅga*; but the door frame indicates that originally it was a temple of Viṣṇu. The Bhumra temple bears on its lintel the bust of Śiva, but the Deogadh temple bears in the boss of the centre of the lintel a figure of Viṣṇu seated on the coils of the *Nāga*, Seṣa or Ananta, exactly of the same type as that to be found in cave No. III (Vaiṣṇava cave) at Badami in the Bijapur district of

Bombay.[1] Some writers call this image the *Bhogāsana mūrti*,[2] but the authority of such a nomenclature has not been stated. The same writer has been misled by the mediaeval repairs to the Daśāvatāra temple in stating "the wide platform on which the temples stand is also sculptured with scenes identified as being from the Rāmāyaṇa. Those reliefs and the pilasters that divide them are a little later in date.[3]" The pilasters and the bas-reliefs in the photograph may be slightly later in date, but the fragment of the architrave bearing a *caitya*-window with a dancing *Gaṇa* inside the medallion is certainly as early as any other part of the temple. The arrangement of the pillars and the fragments of the bas-reliefs along the sides of the platform of the Daśāvatāra temple is certainly not older than the 10th or the 11th century A.D. as proved by the fragment from the *Śikhara* of a mediaeval temple bearing on it rows of stylized *caitya*-windows of the same type to be still found on the *Śikhara* of the great Jain temple on the hill at Deogadh. Fragments of this period were excavated in the compound of the Daśāvatāra temple and two fragments of door-jambs were found by the writer leaning against the eastern steps to the path of circumambulation of the Daśāvatāra

---

1 *Memoirs of the Archaeological Survey of India, No. 25; bas-reliefs of Badami, pl. XVII.*

2 Codrington—*Ancient India, p. xiii, pl. XLA.*

3 *Ibid., p. 61.*

temple itself. The inclusion of the 10th century fragments in the composition of the arrangement of pillars and bas-reliefs proves that this, at least, was no part of the 6th century structure and it is quite possible that the arrangement was done in the 18th or even the 19th century. Therefore these carvings can hardly be called "Sculptures from the base of the Vishṇu temple, Deogadh, Lalitpur district, Gupta, 5th century".[1]

The insetting of the great panels in the Daśāvatāra cave introduces us to the subject of Gupta arabesque and creeper patterns. There cannot be any doubt about the superior artistic excellence of all carvings discovered at Bhumra to those at Nachna Kuthara, Deogadh, and the smaller Gupta temples at Mahābodhi and Sanchi. Even the smaller bands of the door-jambs consisting of super-imposed rosettes or spiral-work cannot be compared with any thing discovered at Bhumra. The marginal decoration of the great panels at Deogadh suffer very much in comparison with the Bhumra fragments. Let us take for example the meandering creeper issuing out of conch shells in the inner bands of the jambs at Deogadh and compare it with the wonderful volutes of the spiral-work of Bhumra.[2] Everywhere Deogadh work lacks the elasticity of Bhumra; compare the fragments of the stylized

---

[1] *Ibid., p. xii, pl. XXXIB.*

[2] *Memoirs of the Archaeological Survey of India No. 16; the temple of Śiva at Bhumara, pl. IV.*

acanthus at Bhumra,[1] and the uninjured mass of the same work at Deogadh.[2] I have not found any parallel to the great spiral-work representing the breaking crests of waves,[3] but even the smaller bands on the sides of the door jambs are always infinitely superior in poise and elasticity[4] to any Deogadh work. There cannot be any comparison with the meandering creeper from Bhumra, the stem of which is hidden among a mass of flowering arabesque, with chubby little climbing *amorini* in the interspaces. Even the Bhita fragments[5] in the Lucknow Museum are stale compared with it.[6] The Deogadh temple is bigger than the temples at Bhumra or Nachna Kuthara and therefore it possesses the advantage of height. Therefore the great pillars of the porches, of which there were four in number, are superior to the smaller pillars and pilasters of Bhumra. But to do justice to the exquisite little jambs at Bhumra one must admit the unsurpassability of the unique geometrical decoration of the inner bands of the door-frame and the wonderful elasticity of the conventional buds of the outer band, both of which bands are continued over the lintel. The poise in the *Kirttimukhas* of the pillars and the pilasters and finally the exquisite group of the prostrate figures below the

---

1 *Ibid., pl. VII (b).*

2 *Ancient India, pl. XXXIA.*

3 *Memoirs of the Archaeological Survey of India, No. 16. pl. VII (c).*

4 *Ibid., pl. IV (b).*

5 *Ancient India, pl. XXXB.*

6 *Memoirs of the Archaeological Survey of India, No. 16, pl. VII (a)*

foliated vase at the bottoms of the fluted pillars have not been surpassed yet.[1] The difference between the work of Bhumra and Deogadh in figures can be neatly gauged by a comparison of the dancing *gaṇa* in the small *caitya*-window,[2] in Bhumra and the same drab heavy figure found at Deogadh.[3] There are no parallels to the exquisite fluted and plain columns of Bhumra in which each base is shaped in a unique fashion. The modelling of the foliated bases at the bottom of the fluted columns shows four slender figures of sprites prostrated by the heavy weight of the urn they bear on their backs, the centre of which is, again, tied with ribands and ornamented with loops issuing from the calyx of lotuses. A fringe of semi-lotus patterns ornament the edge of the urn. Apparently from the heads of the prostrate *gaṇas* rise a mass of ornamental foliage which really issue out of the urn. The conventional varieties of this particular *motif* are more noticeable at Bhumra than anywhere else. In the case of the columns with round shafts, the urn has a narrower neck than its middle and the neck only is fringed with a conventional acanthus pattern; but the place of the foliage at the corners is taken by four projections at the corners, which look more like peacocks with tails spread fanwise, but are really a new style in arabesque.[4]

---

1 *Ibid., pls. III–VI.*
2 *Ibid., pl. VI (b).*
3 *Ancient India, pl. XXXIB;* the *caitya*-window in the upper row.
4 *Memoirs of the Archaeological Survey of India, No. 16, pl. VI (a).*

The art of Bhumra shows the climax reached in the production of human forms during the Gupta period, that of Deogadh the first stage in its decline and the fragments of bas-reliefs at Mundeśvarī the final decline in the post Gupta period of the 5th century. Intermediate between them are the great fragments from Gadhwa in the Allahabad district, now preserved in the Lucknow Museum. In decorative art the Gadhwa fragments appear to be earlier than the earliest period of the building of the Daśāvatāra temple at Deogadh. The climbing *Nereids* in the arches of the meandering creeper are of the Eastern or the Pāṭaliputra school type from the modelling of their torsos.[1] All four bas-reliefs preserved in the Lucknow Museum are certainly older than the oldest work at Deogadh and cruder in comparison with the finished art of Bhumra. The figure work of Gadhwa bas-reliefs is strongly reminiscent of the Mathurā school though in the lintels the special characteristics of the Benares school are seen to be overcoming Mathurā influence.[2]

The remains at Mandasor are still imperfectly known though some of the sites around the city were recently excavated by the Archæological Department of the Gwalior State. The remains were discovered by Captain (now Lieutenant-Colonel) C. E. Luard, M.A.,[3] in 1907 and finally

---

1 *Ancient India, pl. XXX B.* 2 *Ibid., Fig. A, C-D.*

3 *Ind., Ant., Vol. XXXVII, 1908, pp. 107–10, pls. I–III.*

exposed by Mr. M. B. Garde.[1] The pillar at Khilchipura, described by Luard, is certainly of the Mathurā-Kuṣāṇa type, with its super-imposed panels containing figure work surmounted by the ancient Mauryan flat lotus.[2] So also the figure of Śiva from Sondni[3] and the *Dvārapālas* are slightly different from the best type of the Benares school. The *Dvārapālas* remind one very strongly of the great colossus (Viṣṇu) inside the ruined temple at Eran in the Sagar district of the Central Provinces. The affinity between the local products in Central India is further evident in the treatment of monoliths. The great pillars of Yaśodharman[4] resemble the Eran pillars of G. E. 165 and 191. The continuation of the use of the bell-shaped abacus and the pure honey-suckle in the capital on the pillars of Yaśodharman as well as the Gupta capital on the top of Bhilsa hill, the palm capital in the Lucknow Museum all tend to prove the slavish imitation of Maurya and Śuṅga *motifs* in the Gupta art of Central India.[5] The date of the Bagh caves is far from certain and in spite of what Marshall and his colleagues have said in the recent monograph[6] it must be admitted that no convincing proof has been discovered

---

1 *Annual Report of the Archaeological Survey of India 1925–26, pp. 187–8. pl. LXVIII (a–b).*

2 *Ibid., pl. LXIX (b); see also Ind., Ant., Vol. XXXVII, pl. III. 4.*

3 *Ibid., pl. III. 5.*

4 *Ind., Ant., Vol. XVII, pl. I : Annual Report of the Archaeological Survey of India 1925–26, pl. LXVIII (c).*

5 *Ibid., pl. LXVIII (a).* 6 *The Bagh caves.*

which would permit us to come to any reasonable conclusion regarding dates of the painting and sculptures in this series of excavations. The Buddha figures of the Bagh caves[1] strongly resemble the South-Indian type of the second or mediaeval group of caves at Ajanta.

Bagh is situated to the north of the Narmada but to the south of the Vindhyan ranges, a few miles north of Kukshi on the road from Dhar to Khandesh. It lies more than sixty miles due east of Maheshwar, the ancient Māhishmatī, once the capital of the Holkars. Such figures as are still preserved in the Bagh caves show that they are exact replicas of the series of caves of Western India beginning with Poladungar and Dhamnar in the north, and ending with the later caves in the Poona and Satara districts of the Bombay Presidency. Thus the free-standing columns of cave No. I remind one very strongly of the later cave called Jogesvari, near Andheri in the Thana district of Bombay.[2] Some however are fluted but with spirals.[3] In the majority of cases the cruciform bracket capitals are ornamented with the "wing" patterns so profusely used in all three wings of the great cave or Cave No. I at Gharapuri or Elephanta, off Bombay.[4] The later date, than the Gupta period proper, is proved, in the case of all caves at Bagh by the total rejection of

---

1 *Ind., Ant., Vol. XXXIX, 1910 pl. III.* 2 *The Bagh caves pl. III.*
3 *Ibid., pls. IV–V.* 4 *Ibid., pl. IV.*

the apsidal form in *Caitya-Gharas* such as Cave No. I.[1] The only pure Gupta *motif* is that of the *Caitya*-window with circular medallion in the centre of Cave No. IV.[2] So, also, the three Buddhas and Bodhisatvas on the right and left walls of the vestibule of Cave No. II and the two Bodhisatvas in the same cave[3] are of the same type as those at Montpezir or Mandapeśvara near Borivli in the Thana district of Bombay and the mediæval caves at Ajanta. The facades of caves No. II, IV, and V[4] are exactly like the smaller caves at Gharapuri or Elephanta.[5] Therefore, the Bagh Caves, though they are to the north of the Narmadā, cannot be taken to be specimens of Northern Cave temples. Sir John Marshall's opinion on the style of the paintings leave no doubt about their southern origin: "On the other hand, as far as their artistry is concerned, there is little to choose between the pictures of Bagh and Ajanta. Both exhibit the same broad handling of their subjects, the same poetry of motions, the same wonderful diversity in the poses of their figures, the same feeling for colour and the same strong yet subtle line-work. In both, decorative beauty is the key-note to which all else is attuned, and both are as free from realism as they are from stereotyped convention".[6]

---

[1] *Ibid., pl. I.*
[2] *Ibid., pls. VIII–XII.*
[3] *Ibid., pls. VI–VIII.*
[4] *Ibid., pls. II–X.*
[5] *Annual Report of the Archæological Survey 1922-23, pl. XII.*
[6] *The Bagh caves, p. 17.*

Our knowledge of Gupta terracottas is yet in its infancy. Much has been discovered though very little has been preserved. In the last century, hundreds of bricks stamped with the name of Kumāragupta, were discovered at Bhitàri, near Saiyadpur in the Ghazipur district, and removed to the Museum at Lucknow, where many of them are still preserved. From the form of the writing it appears that these bricks were apparently used for constructing some religious edifice in the reign of Kumāragupta I. They are box-moulded and much larger than modern tiles. A carved brick was recently discovered at Bilsad in the Etah district bearing on it concentric circles filled with ornamental foliage and arabesque. This is the most elaborately decorated tile of the Gupta period that has ever been discovered.

Bassi-relievi in terracotta are still very rare. We must not take into consideration the hundreds of thousands terracotta plaques discovered at Bodh-Gaya, Nālandā, etc., where they were left as votive offerings by Buddhist pilgrims. Beginning with the plaque which figures the cover of the Journal of the Bihar and Orissa Research Society, in which Kharoshthi has been used, down to the 12th century A.D., these plaques were cast in wooden or metal moulds and turned out by thousands. Some of them certainly exhibit superior moulding but as a class they cannot be called objects of arts.

The best examples of terracotta plaques, known at present, which can be relegated to the Gupta period, were found in 1926 at Dah Parbatiya in the Darrang district of Assam around the stone door-frame discovered there. Fragments of two terracotta plaques were discovered at this place by officers of the Public Works Departments of Assam. They show the nice poise and the naturalism of the human figure. Unfortunately both of them were recovered in a damaged condition.[1]

---

[1] *Annual Report of the Archæological Survey of India*, 1925-26, *pl. LIV (f)*.

CHAPTER VI.

COINAGE.

Allan's Catalogue of the coins of the Gupta dynasties in the British Museum has thrown much new light on the subject of the coinage of the Gupta empire, so that certain minor problems only remain to be solved, which must await fresh discovery. Earlier writers on the subject, especially the late Dr. V. A. Smith, paved the way for the preparation of Allan's great work, but they were obsessed with numismatic theories, which proved a bar to the solution of the many intricate problems which presented themselves in the last century; such as, a second capital of the Gupta empire in the United Provinces, etc.

With the rise of the Gupta empire there was a reformation of the currency in Northern India and the current coinage was modified by Samudragupta, the second monarch of the Gupta dynasty. Coins of Candragupta I, are known in sufficiently large number but it is extremely doubtful whether they were issued by the king whose name they bear. This idea is Allan's, and his grounds are that instead of being of the Later Kushan type, they are actually of the type of Samudragupta. "The earliest Gupta coins follow the standard of their late Kushan prototypes. Ten well preserved coins of

Samudragupta's Standard type average 118·9 grains (highest 120·6 and 121), four of the archer type 118·1 (highest 120), six of the Candragupta I type, 119 grains (highest 121 and 123), two of the Kāca type (most specimen of which are worn), 117·6 (highest 118), five of the Lyrist type, 118·6 (highest 120·7 and 120) six of the Aśvamedha type, 118·3 grains. These figures agree very well with the weights of the late Kushan coins of the third century which run from 118 to 122 grains. With the types and standard of their northern neighbours the Guptas seem also to have adopted the name *dīnāra,* by which these coins were known to the Kushans this name is to be traced to the Roman solidus. The variations of four to six grains in well preserved specimens of the same type of Samudragupta's coin may be due to variations of the standard in different districts, but it probably shows that little effort was made to strike the coins accurately on a particular standard, and that they were considered rather as medals than coins. This standard may be defined as of about 121 grains."[1]

Samudragupta issued coins in which the obverse type of the late Kuṣāṇa coinage, *e.g.*, the Standing King was copied, but he introduced many other variations into it like Jalāl-uddīn Muḥammad Akbar and Nūruddīn

[1] J. Allan—*Catalogue of the Indian coins in the British Museum–Gupta dynasties. London, 1914 pp. cxxxi–cxxxii.*

Jahāngīr. These are also coins but were struck as memorial medals on certain occasions. "The commonest coins of Samudragupta, the son and successor of Candragupta I, are of the type to which Vincent Smith has given the name Spearman or Javelin, but which may more correctly be called the Standard type. It is evident that Samudragupta's Standard type is a close copy of the later coins of Kushan type, such as have been described by Cunningham (*Num. Chron.*, 1893, Pl. VIII, 2–12 and Pl. IX); practically the only alterations, apart from the legends are on the obverse, where the Kushan peaked camp is replaced by a close-fitting cap, while the trident on the left gives place to a Garuḍa standard (*garuḍadhvaja*), the emblem of Viṣṇu. The king's name is still written vertically; this custom, which was to survive till the end of the dynasty, is to be traced back through the later Kushan coinage to Chinese influence in Central Asia."[1] Along with the ordinary Standard type of his gold coins Samudragupta also issued gold coins of the Archer type, the Battle-axe type, Tiger type, Lyrist type, Aśvamedha type and the Kāca type. Allan attributes the coins bearing the names of Candragupta I, and his wife Kumāradevī to Samudragupta. He considers that these coins were issued by Samudragupta, and not

---

[1] *Ibid*, *p. lxv.*

by his father Candragupta I, to commemorate his father and mother.[1] His arguments are:—

(i) If the coins bearing the names of Candragupta I and Kumāradevī were really issued by Candragupta I then we are at a loss to account for a return "to a relatively slavish imitation of Kushan type after the comparative originality of his father's coins", in the Standard type of Samudragupta.

(ii) "Were the Gupta coins a local development in Magadha of the late Kushan coins, from which they are obviously derived, one would expect the latter to be present in finds of Gupta coins . . . . we must, therefore, place the origin of the Gupta coinage in a period when the Guptas had come into closer contact with the late great Kushans whose (eastern) Panjab coinage they copied; what historical knowledge we possess points to this period being, not in the reign of Candragupta I, but in that of Samudragupta."[2]

(iii) Apart from the initial presumption that the Candragupta coins, being farther removed from the Kushan type than the Standard type, which had no

---

[1] *Ibid.*, p. lxxiii. [2] *Ibid.*, p. lxvi.

predecessor struck by Candragupta I, are later, a careful comparison of their fabric with that of the latter points to their having been struck by Samudragupta."

(iv) "If Candragupta I issued coins it would be remarkable that Samudragupta did not immediately continue their issue."[1]

Allan's contention that the coins bearing the names of Candragupta I and his wife Kumāra-devī were memorial medals struck by Samudra-gupta receives support from other coins' types of Samudragupta, *e.g.*, the Lyrist, Tiger, Aśva-medha, and Kāca types. Of these types the Aśvamedha is also a memorial medal, having been struck on the occasion of the great sacrifice performed by Samudragupta after his campaigns in the north and the south. The Tiger, the Lyrist, the Archer, and the Battle-axe are similarly freak types, struck on special occasions in addition to ordinary Standard type issued for ordinary circulation. Like the Candragupta I type, the Kāca type still remains unexplained and may be taken to have been struck as a memorial medal in memory of a near relative or a very dear friend.

The credit of the reform in the currency of Northern India, therefore, clearly belongs to

1 *Ibid., p. lxviii.*

Samudragupta. Like the currency reforms of Farīd-ud-dīn S̲her S̲háh the new currency of Northern India in the beginning of the 4th century A.D. brought about a purity in the metal. The later Great Kuṣāṇa currency, the coinage of the Little Kuṣāṇas and even that of the Scytho-Sassanians, were for the most part struck in impure gold. At times, gold coins can scarcely be recognised as such on account of the heavy admixture of baser metals.[1] Like the coinage of the Great Kuṣāṇas the coinage of Samudragupta is entirely in gold and copper. The gold predominates and very few copper coins of Samudragupta have been found. The author knows of only two copper coins discovered near Katwa in the Burdwan district of Bengal, which bear on the obverse a figure of Garuḍa on the top and the name *Samudra* in one line at the bottom, while the reverse is perfectly illegible.[2]

The Standard type of the gold currency of Samudragupta bears on the obverse "King standing *l.*, nimbate, wearing close-fitting cap, coat and trousers, ear-rings and necklace, holding in *l.* hand standard bound with fillet, dropping incense on altar with his *r.* hand; on *l.*, behind altar, is a standard bound with a fillet, surmounted by a Garuḍa facing. Beneath the king's arm *Samudra* or *Samudra Gupta*" in one or two

---

1 V. A. Smith—*Catalogue of coins in the Indian Museum, Vol. I, p. 89, No. 14.*

2 These coins were purchased by a private collector.

lines. Surrounding the king's figure is the legend, *Samara-śata-vitata-vijayo jit=āri-pur=ājito divaṁ jayati.*

The reverse is characteristic of Great Kushan or later Great Kuṣāṇa coinage. "Goddess (Lakṣmī) seated facing on throne, nimbate, wearing loose robe, necklace, and armlets, holding fillet in outstretched *r.* hand and cornucopiæ in *l.* arm; her feet rest on lotus; traces of back of throne on *r.* of most specimens; border of dots. Symbol on *l.* on *r.* *Parākramaḥ.*[1]" The variations in the varieties of the gold coinage of Samudragupta are mostly on the obverse, the reverse changing very rarely. Thus in the second type we find "King standing *l.*, nimbate, dressed as in preceding type, holding bow in *l.* hand, while *r.* holds arrow, the head of which rests on ground; Garuḍa standard on *l.* the name of the king is written vertically. The legend on the obverse is *Apratiratho vijitya kṣitiṁ sucaritair-divaṁ jayati.* And that on the reverse is *Apratirathaḥ.* In the coins of Samudragupta the obverse legend is sufficient to identify the type of its coins. Allan divides the Archer type into two varieties for a slight difference in the obverse legend.[2]

The remaining types of the gold coinage of Samudragupta may be called freak types and medals, except the Battle-Axe type which is a

---

[1] Allan—*Catalogue, etc., p. 1.* [2] *Ibid., p. 7.*

regular development of the Kushan standing king type. In this type as in the Archer type the king holds a battle-axe (*Paraśu*) in the place of the standard or the bow. The legend shows in certain varieties the syllable *Kṛi* under the king's left arm. Allan divides this type into three varieties. The first shows the name *Samudra* in a vertical line under the left arm. Surrounding the entire flan on the obverse is the larger legend *Kṛitañta-paraśur-jayaty-ajita-rājā jet=ājitaḥ*. The second variety shows the name of the king in two parallel vertical lines as *Samudragupta*. In the third variety we find the syllable *Kṛi*.[1] In all three variety the reverse shows the figure of a goddess seated on a throne with the legend *Kṛitānta-paraśuḥ*.[2] The rarest of Samudragupta's freak types is the Tiger type in which we see on the obverse "King standing *l.*, wearing turban, waistcloth, necklace, ear-rings, and armlets, trampling on a tiger which falls backwards as he shoots it with bow in *r.* hand, *l.* hand drawing bow back behind ear; on *l.*; behind tiger crescent-topped standard as on Battle-axe type." The difference between this type and the regular types of the gold coinage of Samudragupta is that the king's name does not appear on the obverse at all, nor is there any circular legend. Under the left arm appears the legend *Vyāghra-parākramaḥ*. On the reverse the figure of the

---

[1] *Ibid., p. 14.* [2] *Ibid., p. 12.*

sitting goddess gives place to a standing figure of Gaṅgā standing on her *Vāhana*, a *Makara* and the legend on the right is *Rājā Samudraguptah.*[1] The second freak type is the Lyrist. "King seated, nimbate, cross-legged to *l.*, wearing waistcloth, close-fitting cap, necklace, ear-rings, and armlets, on high-backed couch, playing lyre or lute (*vīṇā*) which lies on his knees; beneath couch is a pedestal or footstool inscribed (*si*)." In this case also there is no king's name under the left arm but it is given as a circular legend *Mahārājādhirāja-Śrī-Samudraguptaḥ*[2]. On the reverse we come across, once more, the figure of the seated goddess facing the left, on a wicker stool and the name of the king is given once more in a vertical line to the right, *Samudra-guptaḥ*. The third class of coins of this type is the *Aśvamedha*: "Obverse: horse standing *l.*, before a sacrificial post (*Yūpa*), from which pennons fly over its back; on some specimens a low pedestal below. Beneath horse (*si*)." There is a long circular legend on the obverse: *Rājādhirājaḥ Pṛthivīm-avitvā divaṁ jayaty-aprati-vāryavīryaḥ*. The reverse shows "The chief queen (Mahiṣī) standing *l.*, wearing loose robe and jewellery, holding chowrie over *r.* shoulder in *r.* hand, *l.* hangs by her side; on *l.* is a sacrificial spear bound with fillet; around her feet a chain (?) extending round spear and on

---

1 *Ibid.*, *p.* 17. 2 *Ibid.*, *p.* 18.

some specimens gourd (?) at feet. No symbol." The legend on the reverse is *Aśvamedha-parākramaḥ.*[1] The name of Samudragupta does not appear on any of this class of coins and they have been attributed to this king solely on the ground of the average weight and the *biruda parākramaḥ*. They differ from the Aśvamedha coins of Kumāragupta I in the *biruda* Mahendra, which appears on the reverse of the latter and the uncertain legend on the reverse of the latter's coinage *Jayati divaṁ Kumāraḥ.*[2] We must now return to the medallions struck by Samudragupta in memory of his parents and his relation or friend, Kāca. The memorial medals of Samudragupta struck in memory of his parents are very elaborate. "Obverse: Candragupta I standing to *l.*, wearing close-fitting coat, trousers and head-dress, ear-rings and armlets, holding in *l.* hand a crescent-topped standard bound with fillet, and with *r.* hand offering an object, which on some coins is clearly a ring, to Kumāradevī who stands on *l.* to *r.* wearing loose robe, ear-rings, necklace and armlets, and tight-fitting head-dress; both nimbate. On *r.* on either side of the standard *Candragupta*, on *l.* *Kumāradevī* or *Śrī-Kumāradevī* or *Kumāradevī-Śrī.*" The reverse shows the seated goddess of the orthodox type but on a lion: "Goddess (Lakṣmī), nim-

---

[1] *Ibid.*, *p.* 21. [2] *Ibid.*, *p.* 68.

bate, wearing long loose robe, seated facing on lion couchant to *r.* or *l.*, holding fillet in outstretched *r.* hand and cornucopiæ in *l.* arm; her feet rest on lotus; behind her on *l.* are traces of back of a throne on most specimens; border of dots. Symbol on *l.*" The reverse legend is simply *Licchavayaḥ.*[1] The memorial medals issued in the name of Kāca are extremely rare, being rarer than the Aśvamedha type. The obverse shows the name Kāca in a vertical line and the type resemble the Standard and Archer types of Samudragupta. "Obverse: King standing to *l.* dressed as in preceding types, holding standard surmounted by wheel (*cakra*) in *l.* hand, and sprinkling incense on altar with *r.* hand." The name of Kāca is written under the left hand exactly in the same fashion as the name of Samudragupta on his regular coins and there is a long circular legend: *gāmavajitya divaṁ karmabhir=uttamair-jayati.* On the reverse we see the figure of a standing goddess standing to the left, wearing a loose robe, holding a flower and cornucopiæ in left arm. The reverse legend is *Sarva-rāj=occhettā* to the right of the figure.[2] Allan thinks that "The similarity of the obverse legend to that of the Archer type forms one of the strongest proofs of the identity of Kāca with Samudragupta. The 'highest works' are sacrifices, and

---

1 *Ibid.*, *p.* 8. 2 *Ibid.*, *p.* 15.

may be referred to the Aśvamedha sacrifice with more probability than the *Sucaritair* of the Archer type .... The reverse legend *Sarva-raj=occhettā*, 'exterminator of all the rājās,' is regularly applied to Samudragupta, and to him alone, in the inscriptions of his successors; it is not found in the extant portions of either of his two known inscriptions, but similar expressions are found in them [1]." In the light of Numismatics this proof is unconvincing, because in the case of no other king of the Gupta dynasty do we find another name of the king under the left arm of his figure on the obverse. In the ordinary type of the coins of the Gupta kings only one name is given under the left arm, *e.g.*, Candra for Candragupta II or Candragupta III, Kumāra or *Ku* for Kumāragupta I or Kumāragupta II and Skanda for Skandagupta. We know that Devagupta was another name of Candragupta II from the Sanchi inscription of the year [2] 93 and from the inscription of his daughter Kuberanāgā [3], but this name has never been used on the coinage of that king. Consequently, it is impossible to believe in spite of the adjective clauses and the weight of Numismatic evidence that Kāca was another name for Samudragupta. We have already referred to him in very rare copper coins of this king.

---

1 *Ibid.*, *p. cx.* 2 *Gupta Inscriptions*, *p. 29.*
3 *Epi. Ind. Vol. XV*, *p. 41.*

No coins of Rāmagupta, the son and successor of Samudragupta, have been discovered and he is not referred to in any of the inscriptions of the later emperors of this dynasty. He was succeeded by his younger brother Candragupta, in whose reign we find a more bewildering variety of coins. Candragupta was the first emperor of the Gupta dynasty who introduced a silver coinage. A silver coinage became necessary after the conquest of Mālava and Kathiawad, where the early and later Western Kshatrapas had been issuing such coins from about the 1st century B.C. The gold coinage of Candragupta II shows a definite effort to leave the standard of the later Kuṣāṇas and to approach that of the heavier standard of the Indian *Suvarṇa*. Allan distinguishes three standards:—

(1) "Of these the first is that of 121 grains in use in the preceding reign;

(2) The second of 125 or 126 grains;

(3) and the third of 132 grains. All these are found in the Archer type."

After discussing the weights of the different types of the gold coins of Candragupta, Allan is of opinion that "It is clear, then, that two standards may be distinguished in most types one of 121 grains and another of 126 grains; the latter, which becomes usual in Kumāragupta's reign, is due to approximation to local standard."[1] The Standard type of the coinage of Samudragupta was not issued by Candragupta II and the ordinary gold coin of the reign appears to be the Archer type. Allan divides the Archer type into two different classes, in the first of which we find the goddess on the reverse seated on a throne and on the second on a lotus. The obverse bears the figure of the king as on the coins of Samudragupta of the same type: "King standing *l.*, nimbate, as on Archer type of Samudragupta, holding bow in *l.* hand and arrow in *r.*; Garuḍa standard bound with fillet on *l.*" The king's name is given in a vertical line under the left arm of the figure and around the flan of the coin is the circular legend *Deva-Śrī-Mahārājādhirāja-Śrī Candraguptaḥ*.[2] Two varieties are distinguished in this class in one of which the string of the bow is inwards and the name of the king is given between the figure and the string. In the other variety the string is outwards and the name of the king is given to the right of the string. In the second class Allan distinguishes several varieties:—

(*a*) King drawing arrow from quiver,
(*b*) King holding arrow in right hand as in class one,
(*c*) King holding bow in left and arrow in right hand, and

---

[1] Allan—*Catalogue, etc.*, pp. *cxxxii-cxxxiii.*
[2] *Ibid.*, pp. 24-25.

(*d*) King holding bow in right hand and Standard on right.[1]

In all cases the reverse legend is *Śrī-Vikramaḥ*. The other types of the coinage of Candragupta II in gold are the very rare, *e.g.*, Couch type:—

"Obverse—King wearing waistcloth and jewellery, seated head to *l.* on high backed couch, holding flower in uplifted *r.* hand, and resting *l.* hand on edge of couch.

Reverse—Goddess (Lakṣmī) seated facing on throne without back, holding lotus in uplifted *l.* hand, resting feet on lotus as on Class I, var. of Archer type; border of dots. Symbol on *l.*"

The obverse and the reverse legend on the couch type are exactly the same as on the Archer type.[2] The next type is the Umbrella (Chattra) type in which we see:—

"Obverse—King standing *l.*, nimbate, casting incense on altar on *l.* with *r.* hand, while *l.* rests on sword-hilt; behind him a dwarf attendant holds *Chattra* (parasol) over him.

Reverse—Goddess (Lakṣmī) nimbate, standing *l.* on lotus, holding fillet in *r.* and lotus in *l.* hand; border of dots. Symbol on *l.*"

---

1 *Ibid., pp. 26–33.*

2 *Ibid., pp. 33–34.*

There are two classes in this type in which the obverse legend differ. In the first class the obverse legend is *Mahārājādhirāja-Śrī-Candraguptaḥ* but in the second it is *Kṣitimavajitya Sucaritair-divaṁ jayati Vikramāditya*. The reverse legend in both classes of this type gives the complete *biruda* or *Aditya*-name of this king. The Standard type seems to have been copied from the Battle-axe type of Samudragupta in which a boy or dwarf appears to the left of the king.[1] The Lion-slayer type of Candragupta II was a freak but widely issued type:—

> "Obverse—King standing *r.* or *l.*, wearing waistcloth with sash which floats behind him, turban or ornamental head-dress, and jewellery, shooting with bow at lion which falls backwards and trampling on lion with one foot.
>
> Reverse—Goddess (Lakṣmī-Ambikā) seated nimbate, facing, on lion couchant to *l.* or *r.* holding fillet in outstretched *r.* hand and cornucopiæ in *l.* on *var a* and *b* lotus on other varieties; border of dots. Symbol on *l.*"

Allan divides this type into four classes. The first class shows a different legend around the flan of the coin on the obverse: *Narendra Candra-prathita-divam jayaty-ajeyo bhuvi Siṁhavikramaḥ.*[2] In this class Allan distinguishes a number of varieties:—

---

[1] *Ibid., p. 12.* [2] *Ibid., p. 38.*

(*a*) King to right but cornucopiæ in the left arm of the goddess.
(*b*) The goddess holds lotus instead of cornucopiæ.
(*c*) King to the left.
(*d*) Goddess holding fillet but lion walking to the right.
(*e*) Goddess seating astride on lion.
(*f*) Goddess holding lotus and fillet.
(*g*) King standing to the right and goddess holding lotus only.
(*h*) Lion retreating.

In the second class the circular legend on the flan of the obverse and the reverse legend are both different. In all varieties of the first class and the third and fourth classes the legend is *Śrī-Siṅha-vikramaḥ* or simply *Siṅha vikramaḥ*. But in class two the circular legend on the obverse is *Narendrasiṅha-Candraguptaḥ Pṛthvīṁ jitvā divaṁ jayati* and the reverse legend simply *Siṅha-Candraḥ*. The coins of the second class are:—

"Obverse—King standing to *r.* shooting lion which falls back, wearing waistcoat with long sashes behind.

Reverse—Goddess seated facing, on lion couchant *l.*, with head turned back, she holds lotus in uplifted *l.* hand and holds *r.* outstretched empty; border of dots."[1]

---

[1] *Ibid.*, *p.* 43.

In the third class of the lion or lion-slayer type we find:—

> "Obverse—King standing *l.* wearing waist-cloth and jewellery, holding bow in *r.* hand and arrow in *l.*; lion on *l.* retreating.
>
> Reverse—Goddess seated facing on lion couchant *l.*, holding fillet in outstretched *r.* hand and lotus in *l.* which rests on hip; border of dots. Symbol[1] on *l.*"

The obverse legend is simply *Mahārājādhirāja-Śrī-Candraguptaḥ*. There is another variety of this class in which the circular legend on the obverse is fuller, *Deva-Śrī-Mahārājādhirāja-Śrī Candraguptaḥ*. In the fourth class of this type we find the king hunting the lion with a sword instead of a bow and arrow. Once more the circular legend on the obverse is exactly as in Class I of this type. The fuller description of Allan is worth quoting:—

> "Obverse—King standing *r.* with *l.* foot on lion which retreats with head turned snapping at the king as he strikes at it with sword in uplifted *r.* hand. Legend as in Class I.
>
> Reverse—Goddess seated facing on lion couchant *r.*, holding fillet in outstretched *l.* and lotus in outstretched *r.* hand as on No. 114."[2]

---

[1] *Ibid.*, *p.* 44. [2] *Ibid.*, *p.* 45.

In the last class or type of the gold coinage of Candragupta II a new type is introduced, which becomes the usual or general type in the reign of his son and successor Kumāragupta I. This is the horsemen type:—

> "Obverse—King riding on fully caparisoned horse to *r.* or *l.*; his dress includes waistcloth with long sashes which fly behind him, and jewellery (ear-rings armlets, necklace, etc.); on some specimens he has a bow in *l.* hand, on others he has sword at *l.* side.
>
> Reverse—Goddess seated to *l.* on wicker stool, holding fillet in outstretched *r* hand and lotus with leaves and roots behind her in *l.*; border of dots. Var. *a* with symbol on *l.* Var. *b* without symbol."

The circular legend on the obverse is *Paramabhāgavato Mahārājādhirāja-Śrī-Candraguptaḥ* and the reverse one *Ajita-Vikramaḥ.*[1]

Soon after the conquest of Mālava and Gujarat, Candragupta II was compelled to issue a silver coinage for these provinces, just as the Mughal emperor Akbar I was compelled to issue a new type of rupee for his recently conquered province of Gujarat. The new type was an exact copy of the late Western Kṣatrapa coinage having the bust on the obverse with the date in Brāhmī numerals, the whole surrounded by

[1] *Ibid.*,

traces of meaningless and degenerate Greek legends. On the reverse the *Caitya* is replaced by *Garuḍa,* the family crest of the Guptas. Even the characters of the circular legend on the reverse was very much affected by the peculiar numismatic alphabet of Kathiawad. This legend is *Parama-bhāgavata-Mahārājādhirāja-Śrī-Candragupta-Vikramāditya(ḥ).* This is variety *a* in the silver coinage of Candragupta II. In the next variety, *b,* this legend varies:—*Śrī-Gupta-kulasya Mahārājādhirāja-Śrī-Candragupta-Vikramāṅkasya.*[1] Inspite of his long reign the number of silver coins of Candragupta II are extremely rare. Some of these coins were issued in the 9th decade of the first century of the Gupta era and none issued in the eighth decade are known, thus proving that while Mālava was captured before 82 G.E. 401 A.D. Kathiawad was not captured till at least 409. What was the exact cause for which Candragupta II refrained from issuing a separate type of silver coinage for Central India, which was issued for the first time by his son Kumaragupta I, is not known to us.

The copper coinage of Candragupta II is much better known and more varied than that of his father Samudragupta. The first variety shows the bust of the king on the obverse and Garuḍa on the reverse with the legend

---

[1] *Ibid., pp.* 49–51.

Mahārāja-Candraguptaḥ. In the next type the three-quarters figure of the king is given attended by a dwarf. On the reverse we see *Garuḍa* with two hands in addition to the two wings. There are several varieties in this type, the distinguishing feature consisting of the presence and absence of human arms in the figure of Garuḍa. In the third type we find the three-quarters length figure on the obverse and *Garuḍa* on the reverse. While the legend on the first and second types is *Mahārāja-Candraguptaḥ* on the reverse,[1] that on the third type is simply *Śrī-Candraguptaḥ*, on the fourth type we find legends both on the obverse and the reverse with the bust of the king on the obverse. The obverse legend is *Śrī-Vikramādityaḥ* and the reverse legend is *Śrī-Candraguptaḥ*. Copper coins of the fifth type show *Garuḍa* standing on an altar with a snake in its mouth and the simple legend *Candraguptaḥ*. On the obverse we find the bust of the king as on type IV, but no legend. The sixth type shows no altar on the reverse but the return of the honorific epithet *Śrī* in the legend, the obverse legend being absent. Coins of the seventh type are very small, being approximately about one-third of an inch in diameter. On the obverse we see the head of the king and on the reverse the figure of Garuḍa holding a

1 *Ibid.*, pp. 52–53.

snake and the simple legend *Candraguptaḥ*. On the eighth type the name of the king only is given on the obverse in two lines $\frac{\textit{Śrī}}{\textit{Candra}}$ and the rest of it *guptaḥ* below Garuḍa on the reverse. In the last *i.e.*, the ninth type the name is still further shortened on obverse as *Candra* and we find a vase on the reverse.[1]

With the reign of Kumāragupta I Gupta coinage reaches the highest point of excellence and variety. The reign of Kumāragupta I being also the best period of plastic activity, the coins of this emperor are individual objects of Art. "The majority of Kumāragupta I's gold coins follow the standard of about 126 grains introduced in Candragupta II's reign but traces of the early standard survive in the Archer type .... A remarkable uniformity is observable in the specimen of the horseman type, the commonest coinage of the reign; twenty-eight specimens average 125.9 grains .... The light weight (115 grains) of the 'Pratāpa' coin is explained by the traces of the original type below, which show that it is some foreign coin restruck, and the unique elephant-rider coin (wt. 124.1 grains) is obviously of Kumāragupta's usual standard."[2]

In the reign of Kumāragupta I the average ordinary gold coin was the Horseman type,

---

[1] *Ibid., pp. 54-60.* [2] *Ibid., p. CXXXIII.*

which was introduced as a casual or freak type by Candragupta II. The average ordinary gold coin of the two previous reigns, with the standing king on the obverse, of the Standard or Archer type was not entirely given up but issued in very small numbers. There are several varieties in this type according to the obverse legend:--

> "King standing, nimbate, to *l.*, holding arrow in *r.* hand and bow in *l.*, as on 'Archer' type of Candragupta II, bow-string inwards. Garuḍa standard on *l.* (*Ku*) with crescent above beneath *l.* arm.
>
> Reverse—Goddess, nimbate, seated facing on lotus, holding fillet in outstretched *r.* hand and lotus in *l.* which rests on hip; border of dots. Symbol[1] on *l.*"

In the first variety of the Archer type of Kumāragupta I the obverse legend is *Vijit=āvanir=avanipatiḥ Kumāragupto divaṁ jayati*, in the second the complete legend is not available but it begins with *jayati mahītalaṁ*, it is the same in the third variety. In the fourth variety the obverse legend is *Parama-rājādhirāja Śrī Kumāraguptaḥ*. In the fifth it is *Mahārājādhirāja Śrī Kumāraguptaḥ*, in the sixth it is *Guṇeśo mahītalaṁ jayati Kumāra* (*Guptaḥ*), and in the seventh the obverse legend is exactly the same as in the fifth variety. In

[1] *Ibid.*, p. 61.

all cases the reverse legend is *Śrī-Mahendraḥ.*[1] The second type of the gold coinage is the finely executed swordsman:—

> "Obverse—King standing *l.*, nimbate wearing waistcloth and jewellery, casting incense with *r.* hand on altar on *l.*, while *l.* hand rests on hilt of sword at his side. Garuḍa standard on *l.*
>
> Reverse—Goddess (Lakṣmī), nimbate, seated facing on lotus, holding fillet in outstretched *r.* hand and lotus in *l.* which rests on hip; border of dots. Symbol on *l.*"

The circular legend on the obverse is *Gām=avajitya sucaritair=Kumāragupto divaṁ jayati*. The reverse legend is *Śrī-Kumāragupto.* Like his grand-father Samudragupta, Kumāragupta I performed the Aśvamedha sacrifice and issued special coins for distribution, which are much rarer than the Aśvamedha type of Samudragupta. There are only two coins of the Aśvamedha type of Kumāragupta I in the British Museum:—

> "Obverse—Horse standing *r.* wearing breastband and saddle, before sacrificial pole (*yūpa*) on altar, the pennons from which fly over its back. Legend uncertain.

---

[1] *Ibid., pp. 61-66.*

Reverse—Queen standing *l.* nimbate, holding *chowrie* over *r.* shoulder and uncertain object in *l.* hand wearing ear-rings, necklace armlets and anklets. On *l.* is a sacrificial spear bound with fillets; border of dots. No symbol."[1]

The Aśvamedha type of Kumāragupta I is to be distinguished from the same type of Samudragupta by the presence of a legend on the obverse, its weight and the *Āditya*-name of Kumāragupta I on the reverse and the weight. Six coins of the Aśvamedha type of Samudragupta weigh 118.3 grains but the first coin of Kumāragupta I weighs 124.5 grains and the second, with a ring, weighs 128.8 grains. The obverse legend begins *jayati divaṁ Kumāra* and on the second it contains the word *Aśvamedha*. The reverse legend on both coins is *Śrī Aśvamedha-Mahendraḥ* like the *Aśvamedha-Parākramaḥ* of Samudragupta.

We come to the most numerous type of the gold coinage of Kumāragupta I, the horseman. In the beginning of this century the Horseman type was classified according to the position of the horse, *i.e.*, horseman to the right and horseman to the left; but at present they are divided into three classes by Allan, with several varieties in such classes. Class I shows the king riding to the right on the obverse and a seated

---

[1] *Ibid.*, *p. 68.*

goddess facing the left holding a lotus with a long stalk on the obverse in the first variety. The circular legend on the obverse has not been completely read. It runs:—*Pṛthvī-talaṁ ....divaṁ jayaty=ajitaḥ.*[1] The obverse legend on the second variety is *Kṣitipatir=ajito vijayī Mahendra-siṅho divaṁ jayati.*[2] In the circular legend on the third variety of Class I *Mahendra-siṅho* gives place to *Kumāragupto.*[3] In the second class of the Horseman type of Kumāragupta I we find:—

"Obverse—King on horseback to *r.* as before, but holding bow in *l.* hand with string outwards and without sash.

Reverse—Goddess (Lakṣmī?) nimbate, seated *l.* on wicker stool, holding lotus with long stalk and leaves in *l.* hand behind and with *r.* hand feeding peacock from bunch of fruit, which in this variety is distinctly represented, border of dots. No symbol."

There are several varieties in Class II; in the first one the circular legend on the obverse is *Gupta-kulavyoma-śaśī Jayaty=ajeyo-'jita-Mahendraḥ.* In the second variety of Class II the legend changes into *Gupta-kul=āmala-candro-Mahendra-karm=ājito jayati.* In this variety the horse is going to the left.[4] The

---

1 *Ibid., p. 69.*
2 *Ibid., p. 70.*
3 *Ibid., p. 71.*
4 *Ibid., p. 75.*

reverse legend in all classes is *Ajita-Mahendraḥ*. Another freak type of the gold coinage of Kumāragupta I is the Lion-slayer type:—

> "Obverse—King standing *r.*, wearing waist-cloth with sash floating behind and jewellery, shooting lion, which falls backward on *r.* from leap, with bow in *l.* hand *r.* drawn behind head.
>
> Reverse—Goddess (Ambikā-Lakṣmī) nimbate seated facing on lion couchant *r.*, holding fillet in outstretched *r.* hand and lotus in *l.* hand or lotus only; border of dots. Symbol on *l.*"[1]

There are four varieties according to differing legends. The legends on the first variety are *Sākṣād=iva Narasiṁho Siṅha-Mahendro jayaty=aniśaṁ* on the obverse and *Śrī Mahendra-Siṅhaḥ*[2] on the reverse. The reverse legend on the second variety is the same but the obverse legend is *Kṣitipatir=ajita-Mahendraḥ Kumāragupto divaṁ jayati.*[3] In the third variety the obverse legend is *Kumāragupto vijayī Siṅha-Mahendro divaṁ jayati* and that on the obverse simply *Siṅha-Mahendraḥ*. In the fourth variety the reverse legend is the same as in the third but the obverse legend is *Kumāragupto yudhi Siṅha-vikramaḥ.*[4] The same legend occurs with slight variation of spelling which

---

[1] *Ibid.*, p. 76.
[2] *Ibid.*, p. 77.
[3] *Ibid.*, p. 78.
[4] *Ibid.*, p. 80.

Allan constitutes into a separate variety. In his freak coinage Kumāragupta I closely followed those of his father, so like the Lion-slayer type there is a Tiger-slayer type also :—

> "Obverse—King to *l.*, wearing waistcloth, jewellery, and head-dress, shooting tiger which falls backwards on *l.* with bow held in *r.* hand, *l.* hand drawing string of bow; his *r.* foot tramples on tiger. Crescent-topped standard bound with fillet on *l.*
>
> Reverse—Goddess standing *l.* in lotus plant (?) holding lotus with long stalk behind her in *l.* hand and feeding peacock with fruit in *r.* hand; border of dots. Symbol on *l.*"

The circular legend of the obverse is *Śrī-mām vyāghra-vala-Parākramaḥ* and on the reverse simply *Kumāragupto-'dhirāja.*[1]

A third freak type, the peacock type, is remarkable as being the most beautiful ever issued by a Gupta Mint master. *Kumāra* being one of the names of the divine general, Kārttikeya, the emperor Kumāragupta I identified himself with that divinity and issued coins with his own figure on the obverse and that of the god on the reverse :—

> "Obverse—King, nimbate, standing *l.*, wearing waistcloth with long sashes and

---

1 *Ibid.*, *p. 81.*

jewellery, feeding peacock from bunch of fruit held in *r.* hand, *l.* hand behind him.

Reverse—Kārttikeya, nimbate three-quarters to *l.*, riding on his peacock Paravāṇi, holding spear in *l.* hand over shoulder (*śakti-dhara*), with *r.* hand sprinkling incense on altar on *r.* (?); the peacock stands on a kind of platform; border of dots. No symbol."

The obverse legend has not been completely read: *Jayati sva-bhumau guṇa-rāśi—Mahendra Kumāraḥ*, while the reverse legend is simply *Mahendra-Kumāraḥ.*[1] There are two other freak types represented by one coin each, the attribution of one of them only being certain. The first of these is the *Pratāpa* type, the name being coined from the reverse legend *Śrī-Pratāpa.* Allan thinks that this coin was re-struck on another coin which was non-Indian :—

"Obverse—Male figure, wearing long loose robe, with arms on breast (in *jñānamudrā* attitude), standing facing; on his *l.* female figure to *r.*, wearing long loose robe and helmet, with shield on *l.* arm, and holding out *r.* hand (closely resembling Minerva); on his *r.* a female figure wearing long loose robe, standing *l.*, holding out *r.* hand and resting *l.* on hip; the two latter appear to

---

1 *Ibid.*, *p. 84.*

be addressing the central figure Garuḍa standard behind central figure.

Reverse—Goddess (Lakṣmī) seated facing on lotus, holding lotus in uplifted *r.* hand and resting *l.* on knee; border of dots."

On the obverse on either side of the central figure is the name of the emperor in two vertical lines. In addition to this there is a long marginal legend which has not been read.[1] The second unique coin is of the elephant-rider type. It was discovered at Mahanad in the Hooghly district of Bengal. Allan says that it was discovered with an Archer coin of Kumāragupta I and an Archer coin of Skandagupta and he is of opinion that therefore the attribution to Kumāragupta I is probable. There are legends both on the reverse and the obverse which have not been completely read. The type is also unique in Gupta coinage:—

"Obverse—King holding rod in *r.* hand seated on elephant which advances *l.*; behind him is seated an attendant holding *chattra* over him.

Reverse—Lakṣmī standing facing on lotus flower, grasping stalk of lotus growing beside her in her *r.* hand and holding lotus flower in *l.* arm; uncertain object (vase ?) on *l.*; border of dots. No[2] symbol."

---

1 *Ibid.*, p. 87. 2 *Ibid.*, p. 88.

The silver coinage issued by Kumāragupta I for circulation in Gujarat and Kathiawad is more numerous and varied than that of his father Chandragupta II. Allan divides the silver issues into five classes of which the first three classes were for circulation in the Western provinces *e.g.* Gujarat and Kathiawad. In the first class we find the bust of the king as on similar coins of Candragupta II with the word *varsha* on the left and degraded Greek letters to the right of the bust. We see Garuḍa in the centre of the obverse surrounded by a long marginal legend:—*Paramabhāgavata - Mahārājādhirāja - Śrī- Kumāragupta-Mahendrādityaḥ.*[1] The reverse legend in the second and third varieties of Class I is exactly the same.[2] In Class II there is no trace of the Greek letters on the obverse and the reverse legend on the first variety is the same as in Class I. In the second variety this legend begins with *Bhāgavata* instead of *Parama.*[3] The Greek legend re-appears in the third class in the first variety of which the emperor is called *Mahārājādhirāja* but in the second variety this title makes way for *Rājādhirāja,* which reminds one of the Great Kuṣāan title *Rājātirāja.*[4]

The reign of Kumāragupta I is remarkable for the issue of a separate silver coinage for circulation in Central India. Though the type is the

---

1 *Ibid., pp. 89–94.*
2 *Ibid., pp. 94–96.*
3 *Ibid., pp. 96–98.*
4 *Ibid., pp. 98–107.*

same as the Western Indian coinage there are slight variation. On the obverse we can see the bust of the king with the date in Brāhmi numerals but there are no traces of the degenerate Greek legend. On the reverse we find the peacock in the place of the Garuḍa. Allan distinguishes four varieties in this class. The reverse legend is also characteristic of Northern Indian Gold coinage:—*Vijit-āvanir-avanipatiḥ Kumāragupto divaṁ jayati.* This legend is only slightly varied in the fourth variety by having *divi* in the place of *divaṁ.*[1]

One other class of the silver coinage of Kumāragupta I proves the great financial stress on the Gupta Imperial treasury. These are silver-plated copper coins of the Valabhi fabric, proving that at Valabhi or in Kathiawad coins of the first class had to be minted on little pieces of copper covered with silver-plate during the reign of Kumāragupta I owing to the scarcity of silver. These coins show traces of the degenerate Greek legend on the obverse and Garuḍa on the reverse, the surrounding legend being *Parama-bhāgavata-rājādhirāja-Śrī-Kumāragupta-Mahendrādityaḥ.* The copper coins of Kumāragupta I are very rare and Allan divides them into two classes. In the first one we see the king standing towards the left with Garuḍa on the reverse. The reverse legend is *Kumāraguptaḥ.* In the second type of the copper

---

[1] *Ibid., pp. 107–10.*

coins we see an altar on the obverse below which is the letter *Śrī-Ku* and the figure of the seated goddess on the reverse.

The coinage of Skandagupta, the last great emperor of the dynasty, is still imperfectly known, as most of it still belongs to private collectors like Rai Mani Lal Nahar Bahadur and Mr. Puran Chand Nahar of Azimganj, district Murshidabad, and many others. Only two or three types of his gold coinage are known, of which the Archer type was the general issue and were coined on two different standards. At first it was issued in the old standard of 132 grains:—

> "Obverse—King standing *l.*, nimbate, as on preceding Archer types, holding bow in *l.* and arrow in *r.* hand. Garuḍa standard bound with fillet on *l.* Beneath *l.* arm (*Skanda*).
>
> Reverse—Goddess (Lakṣmī) nimbate, seated facing on lotus, holding fillet in outstretched *r.* hand and lotus in *l.*, which rests on knee. Symbol on *l.*"

The reverse legend is simply *Śrī-Skandaguptaḥ*. There is a circular legend on the obverse but it has not been completely restored or read as yet. It runs as *Jayati Mahītalaṁ—sudhanvī.*[1] Later on, this Archer type was issued on the heavier standard of the *Suvarṇa* (146.4 grains). In these coins we see:—

---

[1] *Ibid., pp. 114–15.*

"Obverse—King standing *l.* as on early Archer type, but wearing long sash. Garuḍa standard on *l.* (*Skanda*) with crescent above beneath *l.* arm. Eight uncertain akṣaras followed by (—*Jayati divaṁ Śrī-Kramādityaḥ*) (Metre: Upagīti).

Reverse—Goddess (Lakṣmī) seated facing on lotus as on preceding coins. Symbol on *l.* (*Kramādityaḥ*)."[1]

The only other known type of the gold coins of Skandagupta is the king and Lakṣmī type:—

"Obverse—On *l.* Skandagupta standing to *r.* wearing waistcloth and jewellery, holding bow by middle at his *l.* knee in *l.* hand, while *r.* rests on *r.* hip holding arrow; on *r.* the goddess Lakṣmī standing *l.*, holding uncertain object in uplifted *r.* hand and lotus with long stalk behind her in *l.* hand; between them Garuḍa standard. Legend as on preceding type (?)

Reverse—Goddess (Lakṣmī) nimbate, seated facing on lotus, holding fillet in outstretched *r.* hand and lotus in *l.* which rests on knee. Symbol on *l.* (*Śrī-Skandaguptaḥ*)."

The circular legend on the obverse has not been read, but perhaps it is the same as in the lighter Archer type.[2] The silver coinage of Skandagupta is as varied as that of his father. The Garuḍa

---

[1] *Ibid.*, *pp.* 117–19. [2] *Ibid.*, *pp.* 116–17.

type was issued for circulation in Western India as we see the bust of the king surrounded by traces of the Greek legend on the obverse and a Garuḍa on the reverse. The reverse legend is *Paramabhāgavata - Mahārājādhirāja - Śrī - Skandagupta-Kramādityaḥ.*[1] The second silver type is the bull in which there is no Greek legend on the obverse but Śiva's bull, Nandin, on the reverse. The legend on this type of the silver coinage is always defective. The third type, the Altar type, is remarkable on account of the title *Vikramāditya* assumed by Skandagupta in it, because his usual *Āditya*-name on silver and copper coins is *Kramāditya.* In this Altar type the Greek legend re-appears once more on the obverse but on the reverse we see a fire burning on an altar. The legend is very often defective and runs as *Paramabhāgavata - Śrī - Vikrāmaditya - Skandaguptaḥ.*[2] Allan divides the Altar type into two classes according to the use of the term *Kramāditya* instead of *Vikramāditya.*[3] There are two classes in the silver coinage of Skandagupta issued for use in Central India. This Central Indian type can be distinguished from the West Indian type by the difference in the marginal legend on the reverse. The West Indian type of the silver coinage always begins with the word *Paramabhāgavata* and the Central Indian Issue with *Vijit-*

---

1 *Ibid., pp. 119–21.*
2 *Ibid., pp. 122–24.*
3 *Ibid., pp. 124–29.*

āvanir-avani-patir-jayati, etc.,. The Central Indian Issue of Skandagupta are divided into two classes according to a slight difference in the legend. In both classes we find:—

> "Obverse—Bust of Skandagupta *r.*; date in Brāhmī numerals vertically on *r.*
>
> Reverse—Peacock standing facing with wings and tail outspread; border of dots."

The reverse legend is *Vijit-āvanir-avani-patir-jayati-divam Skandagupto-yaṁ* on the first class,[1] and *Vijit-āvanir-avani-patiḥ Śrī-Skandagupto divaṁ jayati*[2] on the second.

With the death of the emperor Skandagupta the great Gupta empire comes to an end and with it practically Gupta coinage also. Skandagupta was succeeded by his half-brother, Puragupta, who issued gold coins only of the Archer type. Like those of his great-grandfather Candragupta II, Puragupta used the *Āditya*-name or *biruda* of *Vikkrama.* In certain coins his name is to be found in a vertical line beneath the left arm but on certain coins the name is omitted. The circular legend has not been completely read or restored as yet. Allan attributes certain enigmatic coins with the *Āditya*-name *Prakāśāditya* to Puragupta and the subject will be discussed below. In the British Museum collection there is only one coin of Puragupta with the king's name under the left arm and three others without the name of

---

1 *Ibid.*, p. 129. 2 *Ibid.*, pp. 132–33.

the king. Therefore this king could not have reigned for more than a year or two. His son and successor Narasiṁhagupta appears to have reigned a little longer as the British Museum possesses 12 coins in all of this king. All coins of Narasiṁhagupta are of gold and of the Archer type which is the only type known from the days of Skandagupta to those of his brother's grandson Kumāragupta II. The Archer type of Narasiṁhagupta is divided into two classes according to the fabric. The coins of a ruder fabric fall into the second class and appear to have been issued at a time of great pressure. The coins of this king are very heavy, being 143.5 to 148.7 grains.[1] The young king Kumāragupta II was the son of Narasiṁhagupta and like his father and grandfather issued coins of the Archer type only. His *biruda* is *Kramādityaḥ* like Skandagupta. Like the coins of Narasiṁhagupta *Bālāditya* the coins of Kumāragupta II are divided into two classes according to the fabric. The coins of the finer fabric weigh from 139.5 to 143 grains; but those of the ruder fabric from 146 to 151 grains. The second class shows a long circular legend *Mahārājādhirāja-Śrī-Kumāragupta-Kramādityaḥ*. On both of these classes, only the first syllable of the king's name *Ku* is legible.[2]

The regular Gupta dynasty known to us from inscriptions and coins ends with Kumāragupta II.

---

[1] *Ibid., pp. 137–39.* [2] *Ibid., pp. 140–43.*

We know now from inscriptions that the reign of Kumāragupta II Kramāditya ended sometime before 157 G.E.=476-77 A.D. and that within three years of this date Budhagupta was in possession of Benares, because an inscription of this king dated G.E. 157-476-77 A.D. has been discovered at that place. Moreover in G.E. 163 Budhagupta was ruling over Northern Bengal and in G.E. 165 he was acknowledged as the ruler of Mālava. We have therefore a series of coins and inscriptions proving that Budhagupta ruled the country from Northern Bengal in the East to Eran or North-eastern Mālava to the West. This king did not issue any gold coins unless we are prepared to accept the gold coins of the very rude horseman type bearing the *Āditya*-name *Prakāśāditya* as his coins. The silver coins of the Central Indian type introduced into the Gupta empire by Kumāragupta I are also very rare. Only one such coin bearing the date G.E. 175=494-95 A.D. and issued by Budhagupta is known. In Eastern India Budhagupta was succeeded by Bhānugupta, who is known to us from the Eran pillar inscription of the widow of the general Goparāja, dated G.E. 191-510-11. A D., and the last Damodarpur copper plate dated 224 G.E.=543-44 A.D. The relationship of Budhagupta to Kumaragupta I has been surmised but that of Bhānugupta to Budhagupta is not known. Bhānugupta did not issue any coins, which have been discovered up to this time.

After Budhagupta the Gupta emperors continued to reign in Eastern India and a number of them are known from their coins only. Allan places the following Gupta kings after Kumāragupta II:

(*a*) Candragupta III *Dvādaśāditya*.
(*b*) Viṣṇugupta *Candrāditya*.
(*c*) Ghaotṭkacagupta-*Kramāditya*.
(*d*) Samacāra-*Narendrāditya*.
(*e*) Jaya-Prakāṇḍayaśā.
(*f*) Vīrasena-Kramāditya.
(*g*) Harigupta.

Out of these kings Samācāra Narendrāditya has been identified with Samācāradeva mentioned as the ruling chief in a copper plate from Faridpur by Mr. Nalinikanta Bhattasali,[1] M.A., Curator of the Dacca Museum. Ghaṭotkacagupta may be identified with the king of Mālava mentioned in the recently discovered inscription from Mandasor.[2] Of the remaining kings Candragupta III and Viṣṇugupta are regular Gupta kings with proper *Āditya*[3]-names. Jayagupta is also a Gupta king, as restored from a copper coin; but the Jayagupta who is known from gold coins of the Archer type is perhaps a distinct person as his *biruda* is not a proper *Āditya*[4] name. Similarly Samācāra-

---

1 *Ephi., Ind. Vol. XVIII, pp. 74–86.*

2 *See ante, p. 66*

3 *Catalogue of Indian coins—Gupta dynasty.* pp. 144–46.

4 *Ibid., pp. 150–51.*

deva and Vīrasena may or may not be Gupta kings, because they have *Āditya*-names but their names are different. Moreover, Vīrasena may be a name without the affix *Gupta* similar to that of Ādityasena in the later Gupta dynasty of Magadha. Vīrasena introduces a new type, the Bull on his gold coins which is perhaps borrowed from the bull type of Śaśāṅka of Gauḍa[1] or the silver Bull type of Skandagupta.

Later Gupta coinage introduces us to the problems of identifications of these kings, beginning with Candragupta III and ending with Vīrasena. Unless some more inscriptions are discovered like the Mandasor inscription mentioning Govindagupta and Ghaṭotkacagupta and the Ghugrahati plate of Samācāradeva, there is no chance of identifying and locating these later Gupta emperors. Allan is inclined to assign the horseman type of the coins of Prakāśāditya to Puragupta, but so long as a coin of this type is not discovered bearing the name of Puragupta it will be difficult to accept this identification. The figure of the Horseman is quite different from that on the gold coinage of Candragupta II and Kumāragupta I. The specimens of the horseman type of Prakāśāditya all show a degenerate horse in which a rider is out of proportion and the

---

[1] *Ibid., pp.* 147–52.

horse a sorry specimen of the die-sinker's art. This certainly shows that these coins were issued at a time when the die-sinker's art had very much degenerated. It appears to me that the syllable *Ru* beneath the horse is the first syllable of the name of some other Gupta king (? Rudragupta) who is not known to us from any other source. The weight of the coins of Prakāśāditya vary from 136 to 146·2 grains which would certainly indicate some period of coinage between Kumāragupta I and Narasiṁhagupta Bālāditya :—

> "Obverse—King to *r.* on horseback, slaying with sword in *r.* hand, lion which leaps at him; bow round his body, with string over *l.* shoulder, Garuḍa standard on *r.*
>
> Reverse—Goddess (Lakṣmī), nimbate, seated facing on lotus, holding fillet in *r.* hand and lotus in *l.*, which rests on knee. Symbol on *l.*"[1]

Long after the close of the 6th century A.D. coins of the type of the Imperial Guptas continued to be struck in Eastern Bengal for local circulation. In weight they did not even approach the Kushan standard of 118–19 grains, not to speak of the *Suvarṇa* Standard of the reign of Skandagupta or Narasiṁhagupta *Bālāditya*, *i.e.*, 146·5 grains. Three such coins in the British Museum weigh 81·7, 86·5 and

---

[1] *Ibid.*, *pp.* 135–6.

92·5 grains. Many such coins have been collected for the Dacca Museum by Mr. Nalinikanta Bhattasali, M.A., during recent years. These coins are found in the districts of Dacca and Faridpur for the most part. In 1925–26 similar coins were discovered at Sabhar in the Northern part of the Dacca district and purchased for the Indian Museum, Calcutta. These coins generally show the figure of the king standing on the obverse with the letter Śrī and a horse, and a standing or seated goddess with a meaningless copy of a legend in Gupta characters on the reverse. The best preserved coin in the collection of the British Museum is described by Allan in the following words:—

> "Obverse—King standing *l.*, holding bow in *l.* hand and arrow in *r.*; on *r.* a horse; on *l.* horseheaded (?) standard. Border of dots. Above on *l.* (*Śrī*).
>
> Reverse—Goddess standing *r.*; border of dots. On *r.* meaningless copy of Gupta inscr. (?)."[1]

---

[1] *Ibid., p. 151.*

Plate I.

Copper Seal of a Kumaramatya of the Gupta Empire, used by a Samanta in the 8th Century A. D. Collection of the Asiatic Society of Bengal.

Plate II.

Front of Garbhagriha of the Temple of Siva at Bhumra (1920)
Nagod State, Central India.

Plate III.

The Early Gupta Temple at Nachna Kuthara, Ajaygadh State, Bundelkhand.

Plate IV.

Door frame of the Gupta temple at Bhumra, Nagod State, Central India.

Plate V.

Stone door-frame of the temple of the Gupta period, at Dah Parvatiya, near Tezpur, Assam.

Plate VI.

Early Gupta Temple at Tigowa, Jubbulpore District, C. P.

Temple of Dasavatara at the root of Deogadh Hill
Jhansi District.
(*Photo by Pandit Govind Malaviya, M. A., LL. B.*)

Plate VIII.

Temple of Mundesvari, Bhabua Sub-division, Shahabad District.
(*Photo by J. C. French Esq., I. C. S.*)

Plate IX

Window in the temple of Mundesvari in the Sahabad District.

(Photo by J. C. French Esq. I. C. S.)

Plate X

Carved door-frame from the temple of Mundesvari
Sahabad District, Bihar
(*Photo by J. C. French, I. C. S.*)

Plate XI

Cave excavated by a Sanakanika Chief during the reign of Chandragupta II (Cave No. 5), Udaygiri near Bhilsa, Gwalior State, C. I.

Plate XII

Chandragupta Cave, Udaigiri near Bhilsa, Gwalior State.

Plate XIII.

Virasena's Cave, or Cave No. 6, Udaigiri, near Bhilsa, Gwalior State.

Plate XIV.

Pillar of Garuda, dedicated in G. E. 165 by Matrivishnu at Eran, Sagar District, C. P

Plate XV.

Image of the Boar Incarnation of Vishnu, dedicated in the 1st year of the reign of the Huna King Toramana, by Dhanyavishnu with the ruins of a temple of Vishnu, at Eran, Sagar District, C. P.

Plate XVI.

Main shrine at Sarnath, as excavated in 1905, back view.
(Photo taken, May, 1909).

(b) Brick stamped with the name of Kumaragupta from Saiyadpur Bhatari, Ghazipur District, U. P. (Lucknow Museum No. B 879.)

(a) *Linga dedicated in G. E. 117 during the reign of* Kumaragupta I, from Karamdanda, District Gonda U P. (Lucknow Museum.)

Plate XVIII

Image of the 24th *Tirthankara* Varddhamana Mahavira, dedicated at Mathura during the reign of Kumaragupta in G. E. 113 (Lucknow Museum.)

Plate XIX.

BUDDHA FIGURES OF THE GUPTA PERIOD IN THE INDIAN MUSEUM, CALCUTTA

From Mathura.

From Sarnath.

From Sarnath.

Buddha in the *Dharma-cakra-mudra*, from Sarnath, Benares.
(Sarnath Museum.)

Buddha in the *Bhumisparsa Mudra* from Sarnath Benares
(Sarnath Museum.)

Buddha in the *Abhaya Mudra*, from Sultanganj,
District Bhagalpur, Bihar.
(Birmingham Museum).

Plate XXIII.

Lokesvara Padmapani from Sarnath, Benares.
(Sarnath Museum No. B(a) 1).

Plate XXIV

Ekamukha linga from ruined temple on the road from Khoh to Parasmania, Nagod State, Central India.

(a) The wounded Yaksa, from the ruined temple at Khoh, Nagod State, Central India.

(b) Image of Buddha dedicated in G. E. 129 in the reign of Kumaragupta I at Mankuwar, Tahsil Karchchhana, District Allahabad (now in the Lucknow Museum).

Plate XXVI.

(a) Image of Visnu, from Cave No. 2 Udaigiri near Bhilsa, Gwalior State.

(b) Nagi, from drum of Maniyar Math Stupa, Old Rajgir, Patna, District Bihar.

Plate XXVII.

Door-jamb from Bhilsa, Gwalior State, C. I. (Museum of Fine Arts, Boston.)

Plate XXVIII

Ananta-Sayya of Visnu, in cave at Udaygiri, near Bhilsa, Gwalior State.

Plate XXIX.

Scenes from Buddha's life, (1) *a*. Maya's dream *b*. Birth of Buddha, c. the first bath, (2) the *Sambodhi*, (3) *Dharma-cakra-pravartana*, (4) The Miracle of Sravasti and (5) *Devavatara*, from Sarnath, Benares (Indian Museum No. S. 1.)

8

Plate XXX

Four principal incidents of Buddha's life (1) Birth (2) *Sambodhi,* (3) *Dharma-cakra-pravartana* and (4) Death, from Sarnath, Benares, (Indian Museum No. S. 2.)

(1) *Devavatara*, (2) *Dharma-cakra-pravartana* and (3) *Sambodhi*, Stele from Sarnath, Benares, dedicated by the Buddhist Monk Harigupta. (Indian Museum, Calcutta.)

Plate XXXII.

The Miracle of Sravasti, from Sarnath, Benares
(Indian Museum No. S. 5)

Plate XXXIII.

Arjuna's penance and departure from heaven on Indra's chariot, bas-relief on pillar from Rajaona, Munger district Bihar. (Indian Museum, Calcutta.)

Plate XXXIV

Arjuna receiving the boon from Siva and later seeing Siva and Durga on Kailasa, bas-relief on pillar from Rajaona, Munger District, Bihar, (Indian Museum, Calcutta.)

Plate XXXV

(a) Scene from Rama's life, deta tched bas-relief from the Dasavatara Temple at Deogadh, Jhansi District.

(b) Unidentified bas-relief on the main shrine, Dasavatara Temple, Jhansi District U. P.

Detatched bas-reliefs now preserved in the sculpture shed at Deogadh, Jhansi District, U. P.

Plate XXXVII.

Ananta-Sayya of Visnu in niche of the Dasavatara temple at the foot of Deogadh hill, Jhansi District.

(Photo by Pandit Govind Malaviya, M. A., LL. B.)

Plate XXXVIII

Image of the Boar, Varaha Cave, Udaygiri, near Bhilsa, Gwalior State.

Plate XXXIX.

The figure of the Earth Goddess on the Bear, Varaha Cave, Udaigiri, Near Bhilsa, Gwalior State

Fragments of two bas reliefs from the Temple of Mundesvari, District Sahabad, Bihar.

Plate XLI.

Ornamental brick from Bilsad, Etah district, U. P.
(Lucknow Museum.)